JOHN DEWEY AND THE WORLD VIEW

John Dewey

AND

THE WORLD VIEW

Edited by DOUGLAS E. LAWSON

and ARTHUR E. LEAN

Southern Illinois University Press

CARBONDALE

JOHN DEWEY, philosopher of growth, change, and experimentation, may long remain one of the world's most frequently misunderstood and misinterpreted scholars. A controversial figure, he lived to see his influence felt in such diverse areas as teaching methods and jurisprudence, psychology and ethics, logic and law, aesthetics and international relationships, religion and economics, philosophy and sociology. He brought about a profound revolution in education, not only in America, but in much of the rest of the world. He has been called by many names—psychologist, educator, philosopher, pragmatist, instrumentalist, socialist, experimentalist, freethinker, humanist, pluralist, evolutionist, naturalist, theist, liberal, radical, reconstructionist, pacifist, meliorist, relativist, empiricist, and so forth. This list could be extended.

It does not seem probable that a valid assessment of Dewey's influence can be made during the present century. It will remain for historians, favored by the greater perspective afforded by time and distance, to estimate that influence from the vantage point of a later era. For the present, the many disagreements will persist. But among those who dispute, there nevertheless is general agreement on some points; for no one doubts Professor Dewey's rightful place among the great humanitarians, among those who hold strong faith in the improvability of social man, or among those who believe in the meliorative powers of human intelligence applied to the solution of man's problems. Nor will anyone question his position among the respecters of human dignity or among those who see man's spiritual nature as thriving best only when the mind can follow its quest without fear and in an atmosphere of free inquiry. Nor, finally, will anyone question Dewey's place among those men of comprehensive intellect to whom we sometimes refer as "world scholars."

But future historians who assay the elements of his influence will seek the recorded opinions of men who, in our time, have known him personally or who, during these earlier stages of that influence, have exhaustively and professionally studied his philosophy and the emerging forces which it has generated.

It was with this fact in mind that Dr. Arthur E. Lean, then chairman of the Department of Educational Administration and Supervision in the College of Education at Southern Illinois University, proposed a series of scholarly lectures to be given on the campus in honor of the centennial anniversary of the birth of John Dewey.

The centennial celebration, which included among its events the series of lectures reproduced in this volume, was jointly sponsored by the College of Education and by the Department of Philosophy in the College of Liberal Arts and Sciences.

The contributors to this publication are well known for their leadership in both educational theory and practice and for their reports growing out of on-the-scene observation of education in other countries throughout the world.

DR. HAROLD R. W. BENJAMIN is most widely known as the pseudonymous author of the satirical and best-selling education book *The Saber-Tooth Curriculum*. Former public school principal and superintendent and former editor, he has written several books and many professional reports and articles. He has been on the faculties of various universities and colleges, including the University of Minnesota, Stanford, and Harvard, as well as the State College of Glassboro, New Jersey; he was dean of the college of education at the University of Maryland and held a similar position at the University of Colorado, later becoming chairman of the Division of Social Foundations of Education at George Peabody College for Teachers. He was a member of the UNESCO Mission to Afghanistan, United States delegate to the second Inter-American Conference on Education in Santiago, member of the United States Educational Mission to Japan and of the UNESCO Construction Conference held in London. Long known as a brilliant and pungent lecturer, he has given major addresses at many leading universities and before most of the leading national educational organizations in this country. He is now on the faculty of Southern Illinois University.

DR. JOHN L. CHILDS, long-time associate and friend of John Dewey, is noted as an exponent of the experimentalist pragmatic philosophy of education. He has written a number of books that are well known in educational and philosophic circles. A political and educational liberal, he has served as a member of the National Commission on Academic Freedom, the American Civil Liberties Union, of the National Commission on Educational Reconstruction of the American Federation of Teachers, and of the American Federation of Labor's Postwar Planning Commission. He was awarded the Order of Abundant Harvest by the Chinese government for his famine relief work in China in 1921. For a quarter of a century he was a professor of philosophy of education at Columbia University, where he now holds an emeritus professorship. In 1951, he received the Nicholas Murray Butler Award for his book, *Education and Morals*. He is now on the faculty of Southern Illinois Unversity.

DR. GEORGE E. AXTELLE is past president of the John Dewey Society, past president of the Philosophy of Education Society, the Middle Atlantic States Philosophy of Education Society and of the American Humanist Association. He is past vice-president of the American Federation of Teachers and past vice-chairman of the New York State Liberal Party. His earlier experience included administrative work in public schools of Oregon, Hawaii and Oakland, California. He was on the faculty of Northwestern University from 1935 to 1942. After the war, he served as chairman of the Department of History and Philosophy of Education at New York University, retiring from that post in 1959. Since that time, he has been professor of Education at Southern Illinois University. He has taught at the University of California at Los Angeles, Ohio State University, University of Minnesota, University of Denver, Michigan State University, University of Puerto Rico and the University of Hawaii. He was Fulbright fellow to Egypt 1952-3 and a Lecturer at Yale University 1957-8. His professional writings have appeared in numerous journals and he has lectured widely in areas of education and philosophy. He is co-author and co-editor of *Teachers for Democracy,* the Fourth Yearbook of the John Dewey Society; he is co-author with Raup, Benne and Smith of *The Improvement of Practical Intelligence.* At present, he is engaged in editing the early works of John Dewey, which are to be published by the Southern Illinois University Press.

DR. WILLIAM W. BRICKMAN is known throughout the education world as the scholarly editor of *School and Society* and of the *Education Abstracts.* He is noted also for his regular reviews of educational literature and for his professional publications, including articles in the *Encyclopedia Britannica* and the *Encyclopedia of Educational Research.* He has edited and co-authored a number of books, one of which is *John Dewey: Master Educator,* originally published in 1959. Dr. Brickman has taught at various universities, including the College of the City of New York, the University of California, New York University, the University of Illinois, Yeshiva University, the University of Toledo, and the University of Hamburg (Germany). He has been a member of the National Fulbright Selection Committee. In addition to his other activities he is at present a professor of educational history and comparative education in the Graduate School of Education at the University of Pennsylvania. He has studied at first hand the educational systems in various places both here and abroad.

DR. ARTHUR E. LEAN has the distinction of being not only a classical scholar in Greek, Latin, philosophy, and the fine arts, but a specialist in comparative education and systems of educational philosophy. He has taught in both public and private secondary schools, has held various administrative posts, and has been on the faculties of Indiana State College, the University of Michigan, and the University of Arizona. In 1957 he became chairman of the Department of Educational Administration and Supervision at Southern Illinois University, later serving as dean of the College of Education from 1960 to 1963. Author of numerous articles and book reviews in professional journals, he has traveled widely, observing educational practices in other countries. He is a member of numerous professional organizations and honor societies.

Douglas E. Lawson

CO-EDITOR'S PREFACE

DR. LAWSON's untimely death in March, 1961, interrupted his editorial work on this volume; after considerable delay the undersigned accepted the responsibility of completing the task.

Although the four major papers in this symposium grew out of the John Dewey Centennial lectures series at Southern Illinois University, they have been considerably expanded, revised and annotated. It was Dr. Lawson's own decision to include my *opusculum,* which was not one of the original lectures in the series.

Especial thanks for editorial assistance are extended to Alimae Aiken Persons.

Arthur E. Lean

CONTENTS

JOHN DEWEY AND THE WORLD VIEW

ONE

The Civilizational Functions
of Philosophy and Education

John L. Childs

JOHN DEWEY's philosophy has borne different names, having at various times been called "pragmatism," "instrumentalism," "experimentalism," "evolutionary naturalism," and "scientific humanism." Dewey, himself, seemed to prefer less sectarian and controversial terms, and he often used the term "empirical" to designate his dominant philosophic interest and emphasis. It is apparent that there are important elements in American experience and thought which are friendly to Dewey's empirical, pragmatic outlook—an outlook which links thought with action, meanings with operations, theory with practice, and which makes experienced consequences the crucial test of both truth and value.

In a series of lectures published under the title *Characteristically American,* Professor Ralph Barton Perry has called attention to the indigenous character of the thought of William James and John Dewey. He observes: "No American philosophy can be said to be purely indigenous, but of pragmatism it can be said, as it can be said of no other philosophical school, that it was and is distinctively American."[1]

In a discussion of American philosophy, Professor Morris Cohen once declared that were the United States to adopt the practice of a number of European countries and establish a national chair of philosophy, there could be only one person named to occupy the American chair, and that person would be John Dewey.

For Dewey, the *empirical* temper and method of procedure carried *moral* as well as *scientific* implications. Thus he concludes the opening chapter of *Experience and Nature,* a chapter in which he examines the nature of philosophic method, with the following passage on the moral significance of the empirical orientation in philosophy.

. . . it may be asserted that the final issue of empirical method is whether the guide and standard of beliefs and conduct lies within or without the *shareable* situations of life. The ultimate accusation leveled against professedly non-empirical philosophies is that in casting aspersion upon the events and objects of experience, they deny the power of common life to develop its own regulative methods and to furnish from within itself adequate goals, ideals, and criteria. Thus in effect they claim a private access to truth and deprive the things of common experience of the enlightenment and guidance that philosophy might otherwise derive from them.[2]

As Dewey conceives them, *empirical* procedures and *democratic* procedures share a common moral trait. Both have faith in the competency of ordinary human experience to develop from within its own movement both its governing methods and its guiding ideals. Much of philosophy, as Dewey interprets it, has been occupied with the effort to give a meaning and a sanction to human existence which it has been supposed ordinary experience cannot provide. In thus conceiving its function, Dewey believes that philosophy has assumed an unnecessary and an impossible role. The role is unnecessary because human experience, equipped with experimental procedures, is able to develop from its own environmental encounters all the intellectual and moral insights it needs. The role is impossible because philosophy has no private and privileged road to the realms of meaning, truth, and value. Moreover, analysis of these alleged transcendental systems clearly shows that they are idealized projections of that which their authors have encountered in their own culturally saturated experiences. As Dewey points out, emphasis on empirical method in philosophy saves us from all attempts to make *reason* and *dialectic* a substitute for *culture* and *experience.* He declares that:

. . . philosophy, like politics, literature and the plastic arts, is itself a phenomenon of human culture. Its connection with social history, with civilization, is intrinsic. There is current among those who philosophize the conviction that, while past thinkers have reflected in their systems the conditions and perplexities of their own day, present-day philosophy in general, and one's own philosophy in particular, is emancipated from the influence of that complex of institutions which forms culture. Bacon, Descartes, Kant each thought with fervor that he was founding philosophy anew because he was placing it securely upon an exclusive intellectual basis, exclusive, that is, of everything but intellect. The movement of time has revealed the illusion . . .[3]

It is important that educationists realize that Dewey's empirical method carries significant philosophic consequences. For example, his empirical orientation undercuts the traditional two-world outlook with its historic dualisms of man and nature, mind and body, thought and action, and morals and experienced consequences. Some of the current attacks on Dewey's philosophy are due either to misunderstandings or to serious distortions of his views, but not all are of this kind. Certain of these attacks are inspired by defenders of established social and religious movements who grasp the anti-authoritarian tendency of Dewey's empirical procedure, and who condemn it because they are hostile to the adjustments in thought and institutionalized practice which it entails. Dewey perceived that modern man cannot achieve unity in his intellectual and moral life so long as he remains half-empirical and half-authoritarian. He worked for a reconstruction that would overcome this historic cleavage.

The positive implications of Dewey's empirical orientation are even more important. His orientation gives philosophy both a civilizational source and a civilizational function. At times, Dewey regards this civilizational function as the heart of the whole intellectual function, and, as he emphasized, it has crucial bearing on how we shall conceive the task of our schools in this period of trouble and transition. I shall let him describe this function in his own words. In his *Philosophy and Civilization,* he declares that the study of the history of philosophy:

. . . exhibits as the work of philosophy the old and ever new undertaking of adjusting that body of traditions which constitute the actual mind of man to scientific tendencies and political aspirations which are novel and incompatible with received authorities. Philosophers are parts of history, caught in its movement; creators perhaps in some measure of its future, but also assuredly creatures of its past.[4] Where there is sufficient depth and range of meanings for consciousness to arise at all, there is a function of adjustment, of reconciliation of the ruling interest of the period with preoccupations which had a different origin and an irrelevant meaning.[5]

Take the history of philosophy from whatever angle and in whatever cross-section you please, Indian, Chinese, Athenian, the Europe of the twelfth or the twentieth century, and you find a load of traditions proceeding from an immemorial past. You find certain preoccupying interests that appear hypnotic in their rigid hold upon imagination and you also find certain resistances, certain dawning rebellions, struggles to escape and to express some fresh value of life. The preoccupations may be political and artistic as in Athens; they may be economic and scientific as today. But in any case, there is a certain intellectual work to be done; the dominant interest working throughout the minds of masses of men has to be clarified, a result which can be accomplished only by selection, elimination, reduction and formulation. . . [6]

The life of all thought is to effect a junction at some point of the new and the old, of deep-sunk customs and unconscious dispositions, that are brought to the light of attention by some conflict with newly emerging directions of activity. Philosophies which emerge at distinctive periods define the larger patterns of continuity which are woven in effecting the enduring junctions of a stubborn past and an insistent future.[7]

A number of basic elements in Dewey's thought are comprehended in this theory of the adjustive and integrative function of philosophy in human experience, both social and personal. I shall enumerate some of the most important of these elements.

This view of philosophy reflects, in the first place, Dewey's belief that *change* is such a pervasive aspect of existence that no philosophy can be considered acceptable which either denies or ignores its reality. Since we live in a world in which change and uncertainty are ultimate traits, the responsibility of both philosophy and education (for in this civilizational task each needs the other) is to cultivate the human dispositions and modes of response which are required to deal with the disturbances which novel occurrences introduce into our ways of life.

This interpretation of the role of philosophy reflects, in the second place, Dewey's functional theory of mind, and his belief that reflective thought originates in a doubtful, problematic situation, and that its aim and its test lie in the effort to resolve these thwarting and ambiguous life situations. It is within the context of these problematic and tensional situations that we acquire the capacity to become more aware of that which is embedded in our experience. Human thought is creative to the extent that it uses its fresh perception of what is involved in our personal and group practices so as to construct more adequate modes of interpretation and behavior. Thus in a real sense it may be said that the culture thinks in our thinking.

This conception of the civilizational function of philosophy reflects, in the third place, Dewey's conviction that problematic situations have both their *intellectual* and *moral* aspects, and that a morality worthy of man must be a reflective morality, and not merely an inherited, customary morality. Just as the meaning and the validity of man's intellectual formulations, or hypotheses, are determined by the operations and the consequences they produce in the matrix of these determinate, problematic situations, so also does he believe that *moral* values and principles should be evaluated by the actual consequences they beget in these disturbed life situations. In other words, Dewey holds that the method of experimental inquiry and discovery which has won dominion in the world of knowledge should be extended in its application and given dominion in the world of values and morals.

This conception of the task of philosophy reflects, in the fourth place, Dewey's view that a democratic society in which government is of, by, and for the people is a distinctive kind of society. One of its outstanding characteristics is that it is concerned not simply to perpetuate its received customs and institutions, but also to foster whatever revisions in its established way of living are required in order to make its enjoyed goods and opportunities more numerous and more equally shared. As some of Dewey's colleagues have observed, a democratic society seeks to institutionalize and thereby to rationalize the process by which changes—even revolutionary transformations—are made in its historic institutions. Hence, its program of organized education undertakes to enlighten as well as to transmit, to reconstruct as well as to perpetuate. For Dewey the principle of "life-adjustment" denotes this creative and reconstructive role of deliberate education.

Finally, Dewey's version of the civilizational function of philosophy defines the supreme human loyalty as devotion to this shared process of discovery and reconstruction by which the values of our common life are made more meaningful and more secure. He believes that both philosophy and education should seek to cultivate the kind of human disposition which does not complain about the harshness and meanness of human existence, but which rather undertakes to discover that which co-operative action guided by intelligence can do to control and to ameliorate the actual physical and social environments in which we live. With the development of tools and language, and the emergence of capacity for thought, Dewey conceives the natural world as having eventually become purposeful; and, through the creative cultural activities of man, the process of evolution, at least in some of its aspects, acquires a mode of operation which is creative from the standpoint of the conservation and the development of values. He has written of the significance of this emergence in his book, *A Common Faith*.

We who now live are parts of a humanity that extends into the remote past, a humanity that has interacted with nature. The things in civilization we most prize are not of ourselves. They exist by grace of the doings and sufferings of the continuous human community in which we are a link. Ours is the responsibility of conserving, transmitting, rectifying and expanding the heritage of values we have received that those who come after us may receive it more solid and secure, more widely accessible and more generously shared than we have received it.[8]

Educational principles and practices have already crept into my discussion of Dewey's conception of the function of philosophy, but I turn now to examine somewhat more systematically his theory of education. In the thought of John Dewey, the educational task, the philosophic task, and the social and political task are intimately interrelated. It is not surprising, therefore, that those who think of education, philosophy, and politics as separate and self-enclosed human undertakings should be confused and repelled by his educational theory and program.

When John Dewey thought of organized education, he did not think primarily of a special kind of public building with its own ready-made instructional materials and patterns of operation. He rather tended to think of a human society existing at a definite time and place and sharing a common way of life. He thought of the school as the creature and the agency of this society. It is organized and maintained by adults for the purpose of nurturing their children in their achieved ways of living and thinking. These adults expect positive results from the work of their school, and they realize that the results which they desire can be attained only as definite transformations or developments are wrought in the lives of their young. As Professor Woodbridge, a colleague of Dewey, once said, the educational enterprise turns the human enterprise into a moral undertaking.

It follows, for Dewey, that parents and teachers can be intelligent about the purposes, the methods, and the materials (or subject-matter) of the school only as they are intelligent about the life of the society which the school serves. All his educational thought is grounded in the conviction that there should be a definite integration of activities within the school with the activities going on in the larger community beyond the school walls. What holds for philosophy, holds with even greater force for the work of organized education: its connection with social history, with civilization, is intrinsic. This is particularly true today, when our country is entering a new age of internal and world relationships.

During the deep depression of the thirties, Dewey remarked that his social conception of education had been accepted by many teachers in only a nominal way, because they had not seriously moved to connect the program of the school "with the concrete facts of family, industry, business, politics, church, science, in this country." [9] He was convinced that American education would achieve vitality only to the extent that its program was developed through significant "descriptions and interpretations of the life which actually goes on in the United States today and which are made for the purpose of dealing with the forces which influence and shape it." [10] No conception of the nature of the educational enterprise could be further removed from Dewey's conception than that embedded in the notion of certain of his critics which holds that teachers should stick to their own last, the school, and leave the problems of the social order to those who have been deputed to deal with them.

The adults of a society, according to Dewey, have to undertake a number of important and difficult things if they are to derive a significant educational program from the raw materials of their own group ways of living and of making a living. First of all, they have to become conscious of these life ways and thought ways. Now these operating ways are so near and familiar that they frequently are considered by those who live in and through them as nature's own ways, and hence without real alternatives. But education inescapably involves communication, and communication involves the formulation of that which is to be shared with others. Since adults cannot communicate that which they do not formulate, it is imperative that they become aware of the meanings and values embedded in their traditions and institutions, particularly at those points of tension where traditional values and practices are being challenged by growth of knowledge, by new inventions, and by alterations in life conditions.

It should be noted, in view of certain criticisms which some have made of Dewey's social interpretation of education, that his method of developing an educational program does not restrict us to the local, the parochial, or the contemporary. As Dewey has demonstrated through his own philosophic and educational constructions, adequate grasp of the present necessarily involves insight into the past from which this present has emerged. Understanding of the present also involves regard for that future which is in the process of becoming a present— a future in our period in which the world relations of our own civilization are constantly becoming more critically important.

But in order to organize a school, adults must do more than become *conscious* of the meanings inherent in their habitual modes of action and interpretation; they also must *evaluate* and *select* from among these inherited and operating patterns of group behavior and belief. Adults repudiate an essential part of their educational responsibility whenever they assert that since education is life and life is education, the school has no warrant for deliberately undertaking to determine the cultural achievements and the social practices which shall engage the attention and direct the activities and the learnings of the immature. Adults also repudiate an important aspect of their educational responsibility whenever they cling to the traditional school program with its ready-made subject-matter and purposes, and ignore the actual transformations which are taking place in their ways of life and thought. In order to educate, we have to select; in order to select, we have to reject; and in order to foster *this,* we have to hinder *that.* For example, important cultural evaluations and selections underlie the present demands for increased emphasis on mathematics, the physical sciences, and foreign languages in the program of the American school. These demands may be warranted—but they, and all other curriculum proposals, should be prepared to justify themselves in terms of existing life conditions, trends, threats and potentialities.

On this question of the inescapable role of choice among human alternatives in the construction of educational programs, Dewey has spoken with force and clarity. I cite one instance. After extended discussion of this very point with Bode and Kilpatrick and the rest of us who collaborated in the writing of *The Educational Frontier,* he wrote as follows in the concluding chapter of that book:

It is the business of philosophy of education to make clear what is involved in the action which is carried on within the educational field, to transform a preference which is blind, based on custom rather than thought, into an intelligent choice—one made, that is, with consciousness of what is aimed at, the reasons why it is preferred, and the fitness of the means used. Nevertheless, intelligent choice is still choice. It still involves preference for one kind of end rather than another which might have been worked for. It involves a conviction that such and such an end is valuable, worthwhile, rather than another. Sincerity demands a maximum of impartiality in seeking and stating the reasons for the aims and values which are chosen and rejected. But the scheme of education itself cannot be impartial in the sense of not involving a preference for some values over others. The obligation to be impartial is the obligation to state as clearly as possible what is chosen and why it is chosen.[11]

The foregoing statement indicates why the educational function and the philosophic function have so much in common in the thought of Dewey. School purposes, school methods, and school subject-matters do not spontaneously identify, define, interpret, and organize themselves. In order to provide a program for the nurture of their young, adults have to pass judgment on that which is established and operative in their society or civilization. They should be particularly alert to those tensional and problematic situations in which inherited patterns of group thought and practice have come into conflict with emerging life conditions. Which means that the task of curriculum construction is never completed, and it endlessly involves educators in the process of making value judgments. In this elemental sense, the educational task is an adjustive civilizational task, and the function of philosophy and the function of education blend in the common movement to make more adequate civilizational interpretations and formulations. As Dewey has stated:

The fact that philosophic problems arise because of widespread and widely felt difficulties in social practice is disguised because philosophers become a specialized class which uses a technical language, unlike the vocabulary in which the direct difficulties are stated. But where a system becomes influential, its connection with a conflict of interests calling for some program of social adjustment may always be discovered. At this point, the intimate connection between philosophy and education appears. In fact, education offers a vantage ground from which to penetrate to the human, as distinct from the technical, significance of philosophic discussions. . . .

If we are willing to conceive education as the process of forming fundamental dispositions, intellectual and emotional, toward nature and fellow men, philosophy may even be defined *as the general theory of education.*[12]

As I view it, Dewey's civilizational interpretation of education suggests that scholars who specialize in the various major areas of human activity and thought should share in the work of cultural analysis and formulation which is inherent in the preparation of the school curriculum. Co-operation of this kind from specialists is particularly needed in this period of cultural transition and transformation—a period in which the task of civilizational interpretation and formulation becomes both more important and more difficult. At the present time, teachers and school administrators need all the assistance they can get as they undertake to develop descriptions and interpretations of the life which actually goes on in the United States, and attempt to understand the forces which influence and shape it.

But to say that teachers need the help of specialists in carrying on their educational work, is not to say that they do not have their own distinctive responsibilities and functions. It was at this point of the recognition of the cultural significance of the work of the teacher that Dewey led the way, and teachers will do well to continue to honor him for this pioneering service. Earlier than most American thinkers, he perceived that in our industrial, scientific, and democratic civilization, organized education could not continue as an incidental human interest and social activity. He rather believed that it was destined to become an outstanding human institution, indispensable to the preservation and the development of our common way of life. It was loyalty to this insight which prompted him to work throughout his life to make the preparation of teachers and school administrators for their civilizational task a recognized university discipline.

For Dewey, the construction and the direction of a school program was an exciting and an exacting intellectual and moral task. He believed that this task could be done well only as those who taught in the school had a creative role in it. He was convinced that teachers who interpret and mediate a civilization to the young should be something more than the mere mouthpieces, the routine drill masters, the transmitters, the testers and the graders of the ideas of others. Dewey emphasized that teachers should be regarded as members of a profession who had achieved competence in the direction of those modes of life and learning by which the immature develop into mature and resourceful members of a scientific and democratic civilization. Method was fundamental in his conception of the teacher's function, but equally fundamental in the professional equipment of the teacher was an understanding of the traditions, the institutions, the values, the trends, the problems, and the potentialities of their civilization.

In short, in the Dewey theory and practice of education, the scholarly materials developed by research workers in the sciences and the humanities are indispensable aids for the teacher, but the last word in that process of providing and directing experience which we call organized education does not reside in them. It resides rather in the members of a well-trained educational profession, working along with parents and the educational authorities these parents delegate to represent them. For Dewey, one of the most distinctive and worthy features of the American system of education is the provision it makes for the co-operation of lay and professional forces in the making and re-making of the program of the school.

John Dewey's Influence
on Educational Practice

Harold R. W. Benjamin

IN THE history of education, the most fortunate professional school men to date have been the Americans of the
generation to which the writer belongs. This is an article of
faith and not susceptible to proof. It should be scrutinized
critically as coming from a prejudiced source. Let us examine
some of the reasons for holding this view.

The Americans of that particular generation were born while
the United States was still a third-rate power, isolated from
European entanglements by ocean barriers, and still suffering
grievously from the wounds of the most terrible civil war of
the nineteenth century. The members of that generation started
to school as the name of Dewey (*George* rather than *John*)
resounded from continent to continent, and the United States
became a budding imperialism. They began teaching in
schools of set-subjects-to-be-learned-for-disciplining-the-facul-
ties, schools that in 1910, for example, were little improved over
their predecessors of 1880. As their country began to use her
newly discovered power-diplomacy muscles and resorted to the
great nations' luxury of the final arbitrament of arms, the men
of that generation followed the drum. They mounted and
rode and drew steel in their people's quarrels. They rejoiced
with their people in their victories. They mourned with them
for their dead. They sang their songs and told their stories. As
they returned to their desks and blackboards, they tried to teach
their people's children the ways of a good life by improved
methods of instruction, by more intelligent organization of
children's motives, emotional drives, and patterns of growth.

The teachers of that generation knew that they were living through a period of important historical events. They saw a great educational revolution taking place. They were in it. They watched it being tested at various times by economic stress, by religious divisiveness, by racial antipathies, by wars of various sizes and temperatures, and by frontal attacks from serious counterrevolutionists who feared and hated the revolution's basic democratic assumptions, as well as by flanking assaults from peripheral jackals who saw a possibility for minor fame in joining a general yapping against anything that seemed new even though its import was imperfectly understood by them.

One of the major influences in that revolution was John Dewey. It is the purpose of this paper to examine the nature of that influence and to assess its weight in producing and directing the courses of the educational revolution. It will treat of John Dewey's educational views and practices as such. The relationship between Dewey's educational views and his philosophical theories is discussed in this series by Professor John L. Childs. The present writer's approach will be the pedestrian one of the school man who served in the ranks of a movement in which John Dewey was not so much a combat commander as he was a banner around which the troops rallied.

We can illustrate the scope of this movement and at the same time recall the fact that it had its beginnings well before John Dewey was born by considering two views of the function of the common school. The first is from the Bishop of London who more than a century ago described the common school as being designed "to bring up the children of the poor in the principles of the Established Church and make them content in that station of life to which it hath pleased God to call them." [1]

The second view was effectively stated by the great Yankee teacher who became the first United States Commissioner of Education. "What we want of the common schools," said Henry Barnard, "is enough education to educate ourselves." [2]

To those who have implied that the educational revolution of the last sixty years has been caused mainly by John Dewey's theories, I submit these two statements. The one describes clearly an institution that is an instrument of a settled power structure. It is the kind of school that every autocracy wants now and has always wanted. It is a school for the pouring into human heads of officially approved facts, and for the modification of human nervous systems to the requirements of officially needed skills. It is the laboratory for the development of faceless non-entities in the service of a corporation or a corporate state. It is the college for the preparation of willing workers who will never organize a union or man a picket line. It is the recruiting depot for the training of nameless weapons-users subsumed under the title of *well-drilled military personnel.*

The second statement even more precisely defines a diametrically different school. It is a school in which the learnings are set by the needs and interests of the children themselves in relation to their communities. It is a school of no official doctrine. It is a school with a flexible timetable. Its pupils assist in the evaluation of their own efforts. Its model of the highest discipline is self-discipline. Such a school is pre-eminently the instrument of a free people who, while recognizing that their society needs enough uniformity of behavior for a minimum necessary security, are also persuaded that their society needs even more pressingly a development of individual capacities, not in spite of idiosyncrasies but by their help. Such a school supports and develops a conviction among its people that society advances significantly only by the maximum cultivation of all the peculiar aspects of its original and creative minds and spirits. Between the Scylla of dangers to its customary routines and the Charybdis of social crystallization, these people more often steer a course by consulting their dreams of a better future than by listening to fears of disturbing the framework of their past achievements.

There were three main currents in the American educational revolution. Although they had many people working in them, there were three men who dominated them, one for each of the currents.

There was first the current of the general liberal spirit in American life. Most Americans who have lived in the period from the last decade of the nineteenth century to the opening of World War II will agree that the greatest single exponent of that spirit was the jurist, Oliver Wendell Holmes.

The second was the current of educational theory applied to

the practices and problems of the schools. Here, without doubt, the outstanding figure was that of John Dewey.

The third was the current of school innovation, the trying out of this or that method, device, or organization to see whether it would help move the institution further along the road of service to its people. To many of the followers of the educational revolution, the dean of these innovators was Francis Wayland Parker.

It is probably somewhat more than a chance circumstance that all three of these men were New Englanders who early made the whole country and the whole world the subjects of their earnest concern. It was certainly no accident that the two of them who were old enough to bear arms fought with distinction in the Civil War. It is also significant that the one who was only five and one-half years old at the time of Lee's surrender should have observed the theater of war in Virginia at that tender age. His resolute mother, in what was a heroic move for that time, moved her family to northern Virginia for the last winter of the war in order to be near her husband's Vermont regiment.

The relationship of Mr. Justice Holmes to the educational revolution may best be illustrated by recalling a few sentences from one of his oft-quoted decisions:

When men have realized that time has upset many fighting faiths, they may come to believe even more than they believe the very foundations of their own conduct that the ultimate good desired is better reached by free trade in ideas—that the best test of truth is the power of truth to get itself accepted in the competition of the market, and that truth is the only ground upon which their wishes can safely be carried out. That at any rate is the theory of our Constitution. It is an experiment, as all life is an experiment.[3]

John Dewey regarded this statement as indicating clearly the identity of the liberal and the experimental mind. He said that the essence of liberalism was contained in the three ideas expressed in Mr. Justice Holmes' statement:

1] Belief in intelligence as the final directive force in life.
2] Belief in freedom of thought and expression as a condition needed to get this power of direction by intelligence.

3] Belief in the experimental character of life and thought.[4]

If we check these beliefs against the educational views expressed by Dewey in *The School and Society, My Pedagogic Creed, How We Think, Experience and Education,* and *Democracy and Education,* we can see how closely the liberalism of Dewey agreed with that of Holmes.

It is difficult to overestimate the influence of Holmes on all the intellectual currents of his time. Shortly after World War I there were many veterans of that conflict who read with lifting hearts his dissenting opinion in the case of Mrs. Rosika Schwimmer. This was the case of an elderly lady, or as Mr. Holmes gallantly put it, a lady somewhat past the usual age of military service, a native of the Austro-Hungarian Empire, who was denied citizenship in the United States because she was a pacifist. At her hearing before a United States district court, she testified that her conscience forbade carrying a rifle or firing it at any human being, that she would gladly scrub floors in military hospitals or do any other menial task to further her adopted country's efforts in war, but that she could not deliberately kill a human being. On appeal to the United States Supreme Court, the lower court's decision was affirmed with Mr. Justice Holmes dissenting.

Stronger than the logic of the great jurist's reasoning, more effective even than his graceful and felicitous style, was a solid fact of overwhelming importance to those young men who had lately fought through the shaded lanes of the Bois de Belleau, the shell-swept streets of Soissons, and the hills of the Meuse-Argonne. That was the fact that the man speaking for tolerance of dissent was the only member of the Supreme Court of the time who had ever borne arms for his country. Here was a tall, old gentleman with long, white cavalry mustaches, late lieutenant colonel of the 25th Massachusetts Volunteers, still carrying a Rebel bullet in his slender frame and proud of it. He spoke with the shadows of Antietam, Ball's Bluff, and Fredericksburg behind him. He suggested mildly that the country's security would not be greatly endangered by admitting to the ranks of its citizenry a lady who held views similar to those of its Quakers. Then he added dryly that the lady's chief sin appeared to be a somewhat closer adherence to the doctrines of Jesus Christ than most of the Court were willing to support.[5]

This is only one of many examples that could be given to emphasize the point that Mr. Justice Holmes led the people of liberal persuasion in this country in part by what he said and in larger part by what he was.

What was he for our generation?

If John Dewey was a banner around which we rallied, Mr. Justice Holmes was a bugle summoning us to action when any battle over principles was joined, calling us to form our battalions and fight. Here was one of his calls:

A man may live greatly in the law as well as elsewhere; there as well as elsewhere his thought may find its unity in an infinite perspective; there as well as elsewhere he may wreak himself upon life, may drink the bitter cup of heroism, may wear his heart out after the unattainable. All that life offers any man from which to start his thinking or his striving is a fact. And if this universe is one universe, if it is so far thinkable that you can pass in reason from one part of it to another, it does not matter very much what that fact is. . . . Your business as thinkers is to make plainer the way from something to the whole of things; to show the rational connection between your fact and the frame of the universe.[6]

If Holmes was the bugle and Dewey the banner, the pioneer type of field commander was Parker. It is certainly significant that everyone called him by his military title just as they spoke of Professor Dewey and Mr. Justice Holmes. Even Jane Addams, devout antimilitarist, called him "Colonel Parker." Some of this ceremonial recognition of his military experience may have been an acknowledgement of the fact that he attained his rank in the hard and glorious way, but much of it was more of a personal salute to the old schoolmaster who was always in there pitching for the team with every ounce of his 225 pounds. He was always ready to take active part in any educational battle or step into any educational breach with the same kind of self-effacement and flaming spirit that he had shown when Pickett's long, gray lines swarmed up through the smoke only to be shattered at the last by the bayonets and gun-butts of men who made the simple choice of death in preference to stepping back from the field-pieces they were assigned to defend.

The present writer once asked a distinguished lady who had studied in Colonel Parker's Cook County Normal School to comment on the old gentleman's chief educational theories and practices.

At first she said apologetically that she was only sixteen and seventeen years old at the time she was the Colonel's pupil. "I really did not know very much about educational theory," she said hesitantly, "and I do not remember precisely what the Colonel's theories were." Then her face lighted and she spoke with sudden authority. "The one thing you can never forget about the Colonel," she continued, "is that he gave you the impression when he spoke to you that you and your problems were the most important things in the world. The reason he gave that impression," she added thoughtfully, "was the simple fact that when he was talking to you, whether in his office or in a classroom or just where you chanced to meet him in the corridor or on the street, to him you and your problems *were* the most important things in the world."

Other testimony, including that of Professor Dewey himself, bears out the accuracy of the lady's observation. Like every great commander, Colonel Parker inspired his associates with the force of his own generous affection. For and from each personality with whom he worked he had the deep respect that has the sovereign effect of "bending up every spirit to his full height." For that chief reason he was a great teacher and a great school administrator, and for the same reason he was the beau ideal of the professional educators of teachers.

In this reference to the force of Parker's personality, we must not minimize the reality, power, and scope of his practical educational innovations. While John Dewey was still an undergraduate at the University of Vermont, Colonel Parker was administering the Quincy, Massachusetts, school system on the basis that the social spirit of the classroom did more than any formal instruction for the child, that children learned more from each other and from the teacher than they ever got from books or formal lectures, that the climate of the school must be one of freedom, and that the greatest educational resources were those of mutual aid, sympathy, and love.

As Professor Dewey pointed out in one of his most eloquent statements, Francis W. Parker never temporized, never used little expediencies, and never sacrificed the spirit to the letter. When the Colonel was attacked for being most completely what was later to be called a "progressive," he always made his appeals directly to the people. He trusted them, he believed in them, and they never let him down. This seemed to Dewey to represent the summit of educational leadership in a democracy. Most of us who are or have ever been school administrators will agree with that judgment.

There were many field leaders other than Colonel Parker in the educational revolution. Looking at the first decades of the present century, we have only to mention the efforts of such men as Charles De Garmo and Charles and Frank McMurry. We can really go back to the last years of the eighteenth century when a great Swiss teacher lived the life of a beggar that he might teach beggars to live like men. This has been a long campaign, extending certainly from Johann Heinrich Pestalozzi to Amos Bronson Alcott and to Wilhelm Rein and all his University of Jena disciples. Horace Mann was fighting in it when he engaged the Boston schoolmasters in combat. Domingo Faustino Sarmiento led many battles and skirmishes under the same colors in Argentina and Chile. People like these and their followers made the revolution. They would have made it if John Dewey had never lived. But John Dewey did live, and because he lived the course of the educational revolution was different than it would have been without him.

The first and probably the most easily observed way in which Professor Dewey influenced educational practice was in his role as a teacher of professors of educational theory. William H. Kilpatrick, John L. Childs, George S. Counts, and William W. Brickman, to name only a few of the scores that could be listed, were Dewey's students or colleagues or both. They in turn profoundly affected the course of educational development through the many thousands of teachers and administrators they helped prepare for service in the schools. Thus the current of educational practice was given a steady impulse and direction it would have lacked without Dewey's clear-cut and sometimes provocative views.

There were many other professors in the fields of administration, supervision, and curriculum development who were equally indebted to Professor Dewey's instruction. Leaders like Ellwood P. Cubberley, George D. Strayer, Nicholas Engelhardt, Harold C. Hand, Walter Cocking, Virgil M. Rogers, William Russell, and Willard E. Givens not only trained large numbers of school administrators but also as consultants, school surveyors, and working heads of educational systems had massive effects on the country's educational organization, methods, and curriculum.

Through such leaders in comparative education as Isaac L. Kandel, Paul Monroe, and Thomas Woody in the United States; Sir Frederick Clark in Britain; Amanda Labarca and Irma Salas in Chile; and the many foreign students at Teachers College, Columbia University, an understanding and acceptance of Dewey's educational views became widely disseminated in Europe, Latin America, Asia, and Africa. Dewey's own travels and consultative services in foreign countries contributed to this outcome.

In a broader but very literal sense, practically every school man and woman in the United States and Canada, as well as many educational leaders in other countries on all the continents, were for fifty years students of John Dewey. They read Dewey's publications, they were taught professional courses by former students of Dewey, and the schools and colleges in which they served were often administered by Dewey's former students. No other professor in American history has had so powerful, so lasting, and so widespread an influence on the whole field of education as had this shy, simple gangling son of Vermont.

In no sense do I wish to imply that Dewey's influence in philosophy was not also a very important aspect of his contributions to education. Other papers in this series treat that area of his work.

There remains here the consideration of a school enterprise carried on by Professor Dewey which is often mentioned as having had an important influence on the educational revolution. I refer of course to Dewey's Laboratory School operated at Chicago for seven and one-half years beginning in 1896.

I do not agree with the view that this school was very important. Except by stimulating Dewey's own thinking and particularly by leading to the publication of *The School and*

Society, his most popular educational work, the Laboratory School did not have any great impact on the course of the educational revolution. The school's supposed influence is derived from the later halo around Dewey's career at Columbia University. There were a number of other schools, notably the Cook County Normal School and such later schools as the Horace Mann and Lincoln Schools associated with Teachers College, Columbia University, and schools of the kind organized at the University of Michigan under Dean A. S. Whitney and at San Francisco State Normal School under President Frederick Burk, which had greater influence and more skillful supervision than did the Laboratory School at Chicago under Dewey's direction.

In this connection, it is a curious fact that some of the most vociferous opponents of Dewey's educational ideas, or what are popularly regarded as his educational ideas, commonly ascribe greater influence to him than do most of his own disciples. You can still meet otherwise normal-appearing citizens in various cultural eddies and backwashes who believe that John Dewey was personally responsible for every sin and tribulation the nation has suffered in the last sixty years, from the high incidence of juvenile delinquency after world wars and during depressions, to the foreign policy of the New Deal or the growing burden of government-supported agricultural surpluses. It is a common cliché, even among certain holders of the degree of Doctor of Philosophy, that every child who is permitted to learn something he actually wants to learn is being headed down the road to an intellectual if not a moral hell by the hands of John Dewey. Even in the city and state of New York, among men old enough to remember the first of May, 1898, the single word *Dewey* will not call forth an image of the hero of Manila Bay or even of a great Republican governor, but rather the sinister figure of a professor of philosophy who is somehow responsible for "my brother's grandson not being able to read as well as I could at his age." This conclusion is held firmly in spite of the obvious fact, it may well be, that "I" cannot read now as well as the average sixth grader and that "my brother's grandson" may have an almost insurmountable heredity of low intelligence. It makes no difference; John Dewey is to blame.

We who had the privilege of being members of that fortunate generation of schoolmen who were students of the charming and brilliant Vermonter, even though some of us never got nearer in our university days to Chicago or Columbia than Palo Alto or Chapel Hill, we happy many knew that John Dewey was not himself an educational earthquake but only the greatest pedagogical vulcanologist of a century. He was not the educational revolution itself, but he was the standard in that struggle to which we could and did repair. He was a banner around which we and our people are still proud to rally.

THREE

John Dewey on Psychology in High Schools

Arthur E. Lean

FOR a long time it has been customary to conceive of a definite and significant hiatus between the end of secondary school and the beginning of college. Somehow or other the student who sits listening to the resounding platitudes of the high school commencement orator in late May or June is thought of as an entirely different person entering a entirely different life just a few short months later as he begins his college freshman year, as if some mysterious metamorphosis has occurred during the intervening summer to transform him from an adolescent into a young adult. And this attitude is strongly influenced by the fact that in most cases he is living away from home for the first time.

Doubtless few who have been through this experience would deny the many differences between high school and college. Ample testimony comes from traumatized freshmen who, after a few months of college work, greet their former high school teachers and principals with questions like, "Why didn't you demand more of us? Why didn't you make us study harder? Why didn't you grade us more strictly? Why didn't you make us write more themes and reports?" (Be it noted that these are the same students who complained bitterly to these same teachers about "overwork" and "excessive requirements" back in high school a year or two earlier.)

But these are differences in emphasis, in degree, rather than in kind. Actually, certain often overlooked factors tend to smooth out, if not almost to obliterate, the sharpness and completeness of the assumed break between the old life and the new, at least with respect to subject matter. Investigations into articulation have demonstrated that much which is studied in the upper years of high school is repeated in one way or another in the first year or two of college.

The phenomenal development of the junior or community college has tended to relate the work of the freshman and sophomore college years more closely to the high school, and many psychologists and others feel that the student in his upper teens is maturationally and otherwise more closely identified with the concept of secondary education than with that of "higher" education (which presumably now begins when the entering neophyte registers for Freshman Composition I.) Thus the junior-community college spokesman may not take it amiss when his institution is patronizingly characterized by the higher educationists as a "glorified high school;" on the contrary, he may feel that this phrase contains a good deal of truth and is actually complimentary as well as accurate.

There was a period in earlier American educational history, just as there has continuously been in the "secondary education" of many foreign countries, when some of the subjects now regularly taught in lower division college courses were offered in high schools. Recent emphasis upon challenging the academically talented has helped to bring about a return to this practice; many high schools, especially in the larger cities and suburban areas, have introduced courses hitherto regarded as appropriate to the freshman and sophomore college years.

It is interesting to note that John Dewey made a strong plea for a specific instance of this kind when, on May 1, 1886, he addressed the first meeting of The Michigan Schoolmasters' Club in Ann Arbor on "Psychology in High-Schools from the Standpoint of the College."[1] This was the year in which the twenty-six-year-old Dewey's first book, *Psychology,* was published (a very un-Dewey-like book if judged by his creative library after 1896, as the late Harold Rugg said), and so it is not surprising that he had some thoughts along this line.

The Michigan Schoolmasters' Club had been organized a few months earlier by teachers from the University of Michigan and the Ann Arbor and Ypsilanti secondary schools. Thus it was notable for its inclusion of representatives from both secondary and "higher" education. Incidentally, the Club has had a continuous existence through the years and is still active today, emphasing common problems of the high schools and colleges. Dewey, at that time teaching philosophy at the University of Michigan, was one of the founders of the Club and subsequently served as its vice-president for two years (1887–8), later being made a Life Member.

We shall resist the temptation to comment upon the reception which probably would be accorded today to a textbook on psychology written by a professor of philosophy, or upon the likelihood that such a thing might happen at all, and proceed to a consideration of Dewey's observations on that occasion. (The companion papers presented on the same program dealt with other subjects, such as English, modern languages, and science, of concern to high schools and colleges alike.)

Dewey begins by professing ignorance of the subject on which he is about to speak (a gambit which, when used by many a lesser man, has promptly lost him his audience); ". . . not only," he says, "have I never taught psychology in a high-school, but . . . I have never been as student or as teacher in a school where it is taught. I may lay claim to the impartiality born of ignorance, and the doctrinarianism [sic] bred of the lack of practice." He then describes the two functions, one direct and immediate and the other remote, of his subject. The former he characterizes as "the precise and accurate training which the mind receives at the time of study, together with the information gathered," about which he proposes to say nothing, preferring to concentrate upon the study of psychology from the standpoint of later life—"that training which puts the mind in an enlarged, yes, in a new attitude to all subjects with which it may thereafter come in contact, whether in the regulated discipline of college life, or in the more accidental and wider education of life."

He now poses three questions which he will answer in order: 1] Should psychology be taught in the high school? 2] With what end in view should it be taught? 3] How should it be taught?

He answers the first question with a dogmatic affirmative, and then inserts a touch of humor: "Aside from the fact that if

I did not my paper would have to end right here, the following considerations have weight with me." Education, he claims, is not complete until the educand "knows something of that intellect which has been receiving the training; of those feelings which form the springs of his action, and of the will which has been exercising itself." Indeed, he freely uses terms such as the soul, the will, the mind, the intellect, throughout the paper.

Just as the study of physiology, for example, does not exhaust one's knowledge of one's own nature, so any psychological subject is treated by a good teacher in such a way as never to lose sight of "the concrete mind, the personal boy or girl . . ." The abstract laws and principles of the "mental philosopher" do not make our good teacher forget the underlying and all-pervading individuality.

Having made his point about knowledge of self, he enters upon a discussion of the adolescent nature of the child during the high school years. He justifies the teaching of psychology at this time, even in competition with the claims of ancient and modern languages, mathematics and history, and physical and biological science, as meeting a definite demand in the child's nature. "No matter," he says, "what one's views about the relations of body and soul, one knows that the average boy and girl undergo a mental as well as a physical revolution between the ages of say, 14 to 17 years. There comes to be at this time something like self-consciousness." Now, with adolescence, begins the child's subjective existence: "the life which recognizes its own unique significance for itself, and begins dwelling upon its personal relations, intellectual and moral, and experimenting with them to get them adjusted in that way in which about the whole life of man consists. . . . These are the beginnings of self questioning; of introspection; of inquiries into the meaning of things, and of one's relation to them."

Dewey feels that the study of psychology at this time of life may, while not explaining all things and solving all problems, save "much waste of mental and even moral force" by providing direction for the child's natural inquiries, instead of allowing them to drift.

But besides meeting the student's "dawning self-consciousness," psychology can balance the relations of studies. The student's pre-adolescent mind cares little for connection or relation; isolated facts are enough to answer his inquiries. But after puberty he must have his facts "threaded upon some principle." Again Dewey disclaims any exclusive powers for psychology in this respect—every subject can and should make its contribution—but psychology should serve as an integrating force, a "bond of union among studies." Thus the student can be led to realize "that in studying mathematics he is illustrating laws of his own reason; that in pursuing geology or botany he is exercising his own perceptive powers; that in history and the languages he is becoming acquainted with wills and intelligences like his own."

Dewey concludes his discussion of the first of his three basic questions with an interestingly dated piece of rhetoric: "At all events, when a youth is studying everything in the world, from yeast to elephants and from bugs to Greek roots, it cannot be out of place to call his attention to the fact that he himself exists and is as worthy of study as any of these things."

His second basic question, the teleological one of purpose in the study of psychology, he answers in considerable detail. To begin with, he claims that this study can put greater meaning into the rest of the curriculum, especially grammar, rhetoric, and literature. Grammar, he states with admirable insight, is a very technical study, leading ultimately into metaphysics as well as psychology, but through the latter the pupil can see in grammar not an "arbitrary collection of meaningless rules" but rather "a reflection of his own intelligence."

As for literature, studying it in connection with psychology should verify it and render it fruitful, he says, for a student who understands how the imagination works, "who knows something . . . of aesthetic feeling and its modes of expression," can read Shakespeare, Tennyson and Carlyle with greater intelligence. A George Eliot novel read by a student who "knows . . . something of the facts of human will, and of social and moral feeling" will be more meaningful. Thus psychology can transform "the reading of literature from a pastime with incidental revenue of instruction into a sincere, critical and fruitful appreciation of it, so far as extends the range of the student."

Dewey states emphatically that this psychological study should not dogmatically communicate a system, not only because of differences of opinion among scholars, but also because the student's knowledge and intellectual maturity are not sufficient to appreciate the truth, even where there is no legitimate dispute. Since the chief purpose of the study of this subject is to increase one's knowledge of one's self—a gradual process in which the individual himself is the prime mover— "to present him at the outset with a chart of himself, formulae, labels, nomenclatures and analysis complete, is to do away with the only object of the study. It is to commit the error of depriving the student of his primary pedagogic right *in re* psychology." (The young Dewey occasionally shows flashes of his future form.)

The second objection to "inoculating" the student with a system is that it inhibits future growth and prevents any new learning. "The cartilaginous portions of the brain are hardened and its sutures closed. One who has been introduced when his mind is most plastic into a system of hard and fast distinctions, cannot lose their impress. All new facts he can classify and comprehend only by their connection with his system. When a new fact appears he does not assimilate it; he takes out his rule and his pigeon-holed box; measures the fact according to his ready-made standard, and tucks it away in its appropriate place."

Here Dewey expatiates on "the cultivation of openness and flexibility of mind." He feels that lack of mental flexibility, of ability to grasp new ideas, "or look at old ones in new lights," is the chief intellectual defect of the pupils he has known. He makes it clear that he does not expect "precocious originality of conception," but hopes that their minds will not be inhospitable or alien to new ideas. Teachers should know, he feels, how to make the intelligence of the average boy and girl more flexible, more receptive to ideas, more spontaneous. And here the study of psychology should help because it "requires in such large measure the self-initiating, self-directing movement of mind. The student's mind is at once the material to be observed and the observer. It furnishes as well the method of observation. The student deals, not with a material foreign to himself, by which he may be hampered, but with himself. He must discover the very material of his study." And he must develop his own method of getting at and handling the material.

Dewey sees the teacher's role as primarily that of awakener-stimulator, even in the face of the student's desire for authority. ". . . the test of the teaching will after all be the degree in which the mind is awakened and is given ability to act for itself." Not, he hastens to add, that the teacher must be a faceless nonentity avoiding positive instruction; rather, "the student must be led to reproduce and realize the material in himself." As in the experimental method of the physical sciences, concrete cases will illustrate what the rules mean, and these concrete cases, though perhaps suggested by the teacher, "can actually be found only by the student himself in his own mind." Thus the study of psychology will make a great contribution to the real end of education—"the securing of intellectual freedom, in its various factors of openness of mind, hospitality to ideas, and ability to move among them unconstrainedly." If psychology were thus taught in the high schools, "fewer of our students in college would be monuments of blank and bland helplessness when a new idea is presented than is now the case." Thus spake the twenty-six-year-old Dewey on May 1, 1886!

We come now to his third basic question, regarding the proper methodology of this teaching. Dewey characteristically begins by defining proper teaching as "such . . . as serves the end mentioned, and whatever other ends are desirable." The individual teacher has the privilege and function of determining specific acts and adapting means to end. However, Dewey is not unwilling to make a few suggestions. He mentions approvingly a certain high school teacher who "merely announces at the end of one hour that the subject for the next day is memory, or feeling or whatever. He does not tell the pupils anything about them; he does not tell them where they can find out about them. But the next day, by skillful questioning, he draws out such ideas as he can from the pupil's own consciousness. I can well believe that with a wise teacher, and small classes, this hour is one of the most looked forward to, as well as one of the most profitable of the whole day. The method has at all events the sanction of Socrates, the founder of scientific psychology."

Here Dewey interjects a word of caution regarding the possibility of "undue or morbid introspection" on the part of the student. If the teaching is properly done, the student's feelings and ideas will be "objective to himself." The teacher must be a wise "physician of the soul." Dewey recalls his previous observations on the study of literature as an aid in this endeavor, suggesting that if the same teacher has charge of both subjects, "why should it be impossible to take some literary classic, and read it with especial attention to its psychological features—its treatment of perception, of imagination, of discursive thought, of impulses, of choice, etc.?" Thus the student combines with his study of psychology the appreciation of style and appropriateness and arrangement of literary material.

Since psychology is above all a personal study, hard and fast rules concerning method are difficult to formulate. Above all, "the teacher must come into the most intimate relations with the minds of the students. Upon this condition depends in reality the answer to the other questions: Should psychology be taught, and with what end should it be taught? Unless it is met there is indeed no especial end to be gained by the introduction of psychology into the curriculum. The student would better confine his attention to the studies which he can absorb once for all, with no teacher standing between him and the light."

Thus ends Dewey's paper. According to the report of the discussion which followed, one older professor agreed "that a share of the public school attention should be given to the study of mental phenomena." He pointed out, however, the lack of textbooks and of properly prepared teachers. And, interestingly enough, he went on to enter a protest against the idea, which he considered to be current, "that the young mind can only be strengthened by original investigation in any subject. Certain things have already been learned, and a pupil's mind may grow by a study of facts that have been given to him." A further comment illustrating the temper of the times appears: "We are subject to certain periodic pressures in which one topic and then another is brought into prominence. A short time since, the sciences were in the ascendant, then the study of English bid fair to overbalance all others, and now we have 'manual training' claiming the ascendency [sic]. The true course, it would seem, is to give each subject due consideration, and not in the excitement of the moment allow ourselves unduly to magnify any one thing." Thus did the elder statesman admonish the young upstart—and, incidentally, expound some good advice for these days of over-emphasis upon science and mathematics at the expense of humanistic and social studies.

Another professor commented, "Psychology should be taught in the high schools because so many of our teachers are prepared there. If we knew more of the study of the mind there might be less of running to extremes." Still another comment was, "As we now lack any elementary textbook of this kind, would it not be well to prepare a pamphlet which should contain the dialogues of Plato in such form as to lead the high school student to begin this study?" (Here the report ends, leaving us forever unenlightened regarding the possibility of Mr. Dewey's seizing the opportunity to "put in a plug" for his own maiden venture into the field of textbook writing.)

The student of Dewey's works will have noticed in the foregoing pages much that is characteristic of the philosopher's early period, as well as many signs of his future development. It may well be that, as Joseph Ratner has pointed out, if we except two earlier articles of peripheral significance, "Psychology in High Schools from the Standpoint of the College" is Dewey's "very first contribution to education proper."[2] Its timeliness today, more than three quarters of a century later, is but another testimonial to the greatness and agelessness of its author.

FOUR

John Dewey and the Genius of American Civilization

George E. Axtelle

AMERICAN civilization is unique. In a real sense it has been a "new beginning" for all mankind. This statement has special significance if we distinguish the British colonies and the United States from the French and Spanish colonies, for the latter were settled by European powers to exploit new lands but the former were established by the settlers themselves, not by the government. In fact they became a refuge for those who opposed the home government.

Connections with the mother country provided a certain security, but were loose enough to give the colonists considerable freedom to organize and control their own lives. Experience in the new land required initiative, resourcefulness and experimentation. The authority of old customs and institutions was relaxed and attenuated. The ways of the fathers might be drawn upon for suggestion but could not be copied under the new conditions. Class lines were weakened. The ever-moving frontier kept alive the spirit of independence and of experimentation, requiring the development of a shrewd sense of reality and of the practical.

While there was no abrupt break with British culture, there was a gradual relaxation of older rigidities, and eventually, the beginning of a new culture. Because space was abundant and physical resources plentiful, mobility—physical, economic, and social—came to characterize American life and there developed the sense of a civilization on the make, of an open-ended world.

The dissolution of class lines was probably the most significant fact in the early development of America. It gave dignity to work and to those who worked. It promoted the spirit of enterprise and of hope. It created an atmosphere in which invention and technology had scope and promise. The fact that America was for decades a beacon to millions of poor and discontented suggests the human significance of this new world in the making.

De Toqueville noted the facility with which Americans created voluntary organizations and developed various agencies and institutions to promote their common interests. The New England town meeting was a good example of the way Americans voluntarily joined together in both economic and civic enterprises. The lack of political absolutism freed them for an eventual escape from intellectual absolutism. Life was something to experiment with and to try out for new possibilities.

As an indigenous civilization was being developed in this country, European customs and institutions were transformed from absolute authorities into useful resources.

It is a matter of interest that the literary and intellectual culture was least affected by the new conditions. Literary people and intellectuals sought patterns in the older countries. Not until mid-nineteenth century did such figures as Hawthorne, Whitman, Poe, and Melville begin to write in the American idiom. Since then, our literature has been distinctively American. However, philosophy continued throughout the last century to look abroad for its models and little of originality or distinction appeared.

Toward the end of the century, Peirce, James and Dewey began to give philosophic expression to the American culture and mentality. All three were born and grew up in America; they acknowledged their American heritage and their writings embodied it. Dewey responded more directly and more comprehensively to the American scene than any other. He not only expressed the American genius, he expressed his own genius in doing so.

Dewey was by no means a chauvinist. He was discriminating in his appreciation of American life. He did not confuse the qualities of America with the laws of nature. He saw ignorance, prejudice, poverty, exploitation, and ugliness; but he also saw what was fresh, creative, humane and lovely. He saw America's resources and its liabilities: the liabilities were problems to be solved and the resources were possibilities to be extended and made secure for all men.

THE DEMOCRATIC IDEA AND IDEAL. Dewey was a many-faceted writer. A number of themes permeated nearly everything he wrote. These were so organically interconnected that it is difficult to discuss one without involving the others. However, in all his writings, one is impressed by his concern with man, both in the singular and the collective. Whether he is writing on logic, epistemology, metaphysics, psychology, or politics, the moral-political is close to the heart of what he has to say. In *Experience and Nature* he says that "nothing but the best, the richest and the fullest experience possible is good enough for man."[1] Again, he writes, "shared experience is the greatest of human goods."[2] One might almost say his whole philosophy is anthropomorphic. It is human-centered.

For Dewey, democracy was a mode of associated living which involved mutuality, common purposes, shared interests. He conceived man as a social creature, both shaped by and shaping his social and physical environment. Through the development of communication, man became human, for by means of communication he was able to join with his fellows in common purposes and enterprises and hence to build cultures. Communication not only made associated life possible, it supplied the necessary condition for discourse, for reflective thinking far beyond that of any other creature. It is for this reason that he writes, "of all affairs communication is the most wonderful."[3]

Long before the new beginning in America, in early transitions from tribal life to civil societies, organized cities, states and empires, social life had become stratified into layers of classes and authorities. At the bottom was the great mass of men who labored and drudged, lived and died to serve the ends of those above them. This fundamental fact shaped not only all social institutions but all intellectual life as well. Science, religion, philosophy and politics were in effect both explanatory and justificatory of prevailing institutions, which were considered to exemplify and express the very laws of God and nature. True, Athens had experimented with democracy for a time, but slavery, extreme individualism and exploitation of allies and colonies spelled her downfall—and that of democracy.

The older stratified societies saw the universe as essentially finished in its fundamental features. Species and classes of both natural and social phenomena were considered eternal. Plato and Aristotle, for example, conceived of novelty, change and chance as essentially irrational and unintelligible. Much of Western thought has scarcely challenged this conception. The fact that America was in many ways a democratic, open society, one of experiment and novelty, of social mobility, required an intellectual orientation that was relevant to its character; the cultural new beginning required a corresponding intellectual new beginning. This Dewey undertook to effect. In doing so, he had to re-examine and reconstruct much of the philosophic tradition. His awareness of the open character of American society accounts for his originality and novelty in that reconstruction.

This separation of ruled from rulers had long divided the intellectual universe into non-communicating compartments or dualisms. Among these were experience and nature, man and nature, nature and supernature, mind and body, thought and action, theory and practice, means and ends, labor and leisure, art and the commonplace, the individual and society. Much of his criticism of the philosophic tradition is centered in his attack on such dualisms.

When men govern themselves with common purposes and common interests, there is no necessary opposition between individual and society. Rather, men have both an individual and a social character, with individual and social qualities fused. In such a society, ends are within action rather than imposed from without. Means and ends are continuous in the sense that an end is but a more remote means. Once an end is achieved, it serves as a means to further ends.

The means-consequence continuum is endless. The only way an end can be evaluated is to note the consequences which would flow from it—in other words, the range of more remote ends or preferences or values which it would effect. In short, an end can be judged only as we see it in its capacity as means, not to one end alone, but to the whole realm of ends.

Under such circumstances, labor itself becomes motivated by purpose and governed by thought. The dualism of labor and leisure disappears. Even in our "leisure" we may work—or play. An amateur musician, artist, scientist, policitian or whatever, *works* at his avocation if he *cares* about it. So our play, although spontaneous, may also be serious. Under such circumstances, the real alternatives become capriciousness and responsibility. The one is thoughtless, careless of consequences; the other is thoughtful, concerned for consequences.

Dewey is, without doubt, *the* philosopher of democracy. Everything he wrote has contributed, directly or indirectly, to the clarification and elaboration of the democratic idea. A. N. Whitehead has written, "We are living in the midst of the period subject to Dewey's influence."[4] I suspect that this period will continue for decades if not centuries. His work will continue to be significant as long as men struggle for freedom and justice.

The first item on the agenda of world affairs is the transition from authoritarian societies to those which acknowledge human experience as the ultimate source and test of knowledge and values. Just as this transition involves a reconstruction of social institutions and human relations, it also involves a thoroughgoing reconstruction of ideas and ideals. Just as the rise of modern science from Bacon and Descartes to the present set the theme of modern philosophy, particularly the problem of knowledge, so the American democratic experiment will doubtless set the theme of philosophic discourse for generations to come.

The real choice in the world today is not between communism and capitalism, but rather between authoritarianism and democracy. The "free" world would be in a vastly stronger position if it were not so encumbered with its own forms of authoritarianism. Democracy as a way of life is still groping its way. There are still many hangovers from earlier modes of life and thought which complicate the democratic process. Moreover, the institutions and modes of thought which served democracy well in the eighteenth and early nineteenth centuries are no longer adequate in an industrial society. Finally, the way of life which is democracy is so closely concerned with every aspect of life that nothing less than an all-embracing philosophy can guide and serve the cause of democracy.

Democracy was for Dewey the comprehensive ideal. To understand his idea and ideal of democracy one must understand his conception of ideals generally. Ideals are something more than creatures of the imagination or of abstract thought. To be effective an ideal must be grounded in the world of experience. One must experience an ideal quality and recognize it as ideal; this experience then becomes a criterion by which we judge other experiences. It also becomes a stimulus to make this quality characteristic of experience generally, for all men. Only such ideals are really effective as ideals, for they are perceptions of *real* possibilities.

Democracy is therefore something much more than a dream. Democracy as an ideal has its ground in the qualities which men actually have experienced, and which serve as criteria for judging other experiences.

DEWEY'S CONCEPT OF THE DEMOCRATIC IDEA AND OF PHILOSOPHY. "Philosophy recovers itself when it ceases to be a device for dealing with the problems of philosophers and becomes a method, cultivated by philosophers, for dealing with the problems of men."[5]

Dewey denied that philosophy has special access to "ultimate reality" or needed to have. Philosophy as he conceived it is not a special subject-matter with exclusive jurisdiction. On the contrary, philosophy is criticism, or as he put it, "criticism of criticisms." Its function is to develop critical method for dealing with the human problems of this life.

Conscience in morals, taste in fine arts, and conviction in beliefs pass insensibly into critical judgments; the latter pass also into a more and more generalized form of criticism called philosophy.[6] . . . philosophy is inherently criticism, having its distinctive position among various modes of criticism in its generality; a criticism of criticisms, as it were. Criticism is discriminating judgment, careful appraisal, and judgment is appropriately termed criticism wherever the subject-matter of discrimination concerns goods or values.[7]

Dewey emphasized the role of education in the realization and maintenance of democracy. We see this particularly in his definition of philosophy in *Democracy and Education*.

Philosophic thinking has for its differentia the fact that the uncertainties with which it deals are found in widespread social conditions and aims, consisting in a conflict of organized interests and institutional claims. Since the only way of bringing about a harmonious readjustment of the opposed tendencies is through a modification of emotional and intellectual disposition, philosophy is at once an explicit formulation of the various interests of life and a propounding of points of view and methods through which a better balance of interests may be effected. Since education is the process through which the needed transformation may be accomplished and not remain a mere hypothesis as to what is desirable, we reach a justification of the statement that philosophy is the theory of education as a deliberately conducted practice.[8]

Dewey had a profound sense of the practical, of the *really* possible. He was inhospitable to abstract and wholesale ideas. He was concerned that an idea be grounded in experience. For this reason, he took the sciences as his ideal of the method of knowing, for they not only begin with empirical fact, they also end in empirical fact.

As radically as his own philosophy departed from the philosophic tradition, there were few philosophers who were more conscientious students of that tradition. He studied it scrupulously in order to make use of its almost inexhaustible resources. He conceived philosophy as a method of dealing with the problems of men; a method of effecting a junction of the new and the old.

Philosophy thus sustains the closest connection with the history of culture, with the succession of changes in civilization. It is fed by the streams of tradition, traced at critical moments to their sources in order that the current may receive a new direction; it is fertilized by the ferment of new inventions in industry, new explorations of the globe, new discoveries in science.[9]

[It] marks a change of culture. In forming patterns to be conformed to in future thought and action, it is additive and transforming in its rôle in the history of civilization. Man states anything at his peril; once stated, it occupies a place in a new perspective; it attains a permanence which does not belong to its existence; it enters provokingly into wont and use; it points in a troubling way to need of new endeavors.[10]

METAPHYSICS. For Dewey, metaphysics is a ground map of existence, an effort to designate and explore generic traits; however, its conclusions are as much subject to empirical test as are those of the sciences. The traits of existence are not found in water-tight compartments but are, rather, aspects or qualities which interpenetrate and interfuse one another. A distinctive characteristic of Dewey's thought is its organic quality. He speaks of qualities rather than separate substances or realms of existence. His thinking might be called aspectual, rather than elemental or substantial.

His most general subject matter is experience-and-nature. Experience results from the interaction of the human organism and its environment. Experience occurs in nature, and nature is its subject matter, its content. Experience and nature include everything we can talk about intelligibly. This is not to say the two terms are synonymous, for indeed there are many things in nature of which we may have no experience. Nor is experience individualistic; it is a cultural as much as an individual phenomenon. The culture nourishes the individual as the individual enriches the culture.

The continuous interaction of organism and environment is a pervasive character of experience. The organism not only lives *in* an environment, it lives by means of it. Dewey returns again and again to this concept of continuous interaction; it might be said to be his ultimate reference. All man's activities—intellectual, artistic-aesthetic, practical, socio-moral, educational, religious—take their departure from this fact.

Dewey stated the principle that things exist in association with other things. Nothing exists in isolation. We can know any thing only in terms of the influences it exerts and those played upon it. Action is transaction, reciprocal. The idea of an actor as an initial source of action or actions without reciprocal reaction, such as the idea of the separate, self-contained individual, is a form of occultism.

Yet, things are also individual, unique, novel. No two events or phenomena are identical. Variety, novelty, individuality are the stuff of experience. At the human level, culture is the name for the consequence of the interactions and transactions of the individual members of a region. The culture shapes the individual, and the individual in turn exerts influence upon his culture. Individuality is itself possible only in association. The individual is what he is because of his social relations. Not only is there no conflict between the individual and the social, they are inseparable.

To understand an event, object, person or statement, it must be seen in context. Its full character or meaning can be determined only in terms of its associations, its relations to its context, or environment. Since these are inexhaustible, any judgment must be taken as an approximation. Later experience may reveal other significant connections which must be taken into account.

Some associations are more stable than others, such as molecules, organisms, institutions, states, societies and cultures. A biological organism is a sort of paradigm of other forms of association. Its members are so interrelated that they tend to maintain a definite pattern of organization, yet grow and multiply. They are interdependent in such a way that they mutually sustain and support the system as a whole. A change in one tends to alter the state of the others in such a way as to maintain a new equilibrium. Equilibrium is never static but always moving, changing. But the equilibrium of the organism is not only an internal equilibrium, it is at the same time an equilibrium of organism and environment. It is difficult to draw a sharp boundary between organism and environment. When do the materials of the environment, as they nourish the organism, become organism and cease to be environment? When do waste products cease to be a part of the organism and become environment?

The mystery of the living organism is not only one of life, but of the nature of existence itself. Things behave differently in one association from the way they behave in another. An iron or oxygen molecule behaves differently in the environment of an organism than it does outside that environment; it takes on a different character. As things become associated in new patterns, new creatures appear. Nature is not something created at a particular time in a definite and static pattern. Nature is creative, open, unfinished. The creatures which can form effective relations with their environment endure; how long they endure depends on how well they can continue to maintain effective relations with an environment which is also under-going change.

In short, this is an evolutionary, creative world. As new creatures emerge, they change the environment for others, and in turn have to make new accommodations with their environments. The principles of change and accommodation are particularly true of human culture. The emergence of the alphabet, the decimal system, the printing press had rever-berating effects upon the whole culture. As Carlyle said, given the printing press, democracy was inevitable. We might also say given the internal combustion engine or the dynamo, the whole pattern of modern life became altered. The introduction of a new factor into a system has effects throughout the system. There is no finality; the problem of maintaining dynamic equilibrium with the environment is never-ending.

Similarly, progress is not a unilateral affair of more and more or better and better with respect to some particular standard of good. Within a particular system there may be progress in the elaboration and perfecting of the system, but there is continuous transformation from system to system. The feudal system gave way to early modern; it to the industrial revolution of the eighteenth and early nineteenth centuries; it to the cosmopolitan advanced scientific technology of today. Progress requires that organisms, institutions, societies, continuously improve their relations with their environment.

With regard to individuals, it should be noted that there are varying levels of individuality. In one context the electron may be the individual, in another the atom or the molecule; a higher levels, the protein molecule, the organ, the organism; at still higher, the individual person, the institution, the society, the state, the civilization. Save for primordial individuals at the lowest levels and at the most comprehensive, the universe, every individual both contains or embraces individuals or members of lower levels, and is itself a member of an individual or of several individuals of higher levels.

There are countless levels and types of organization. Each chemical substance has its characteristic type of organization as does each species of living things. So also do societies, although no two are identical. Organizations differ not only in type but in level of organization, or degree of complexity. However, we may designate three major levels of organization, within which there are countless other levels. These are the inorganic, living and cultural. Living structures are characterized by sensibility, need, desire and satisfaction. We can say little about the nature of the consciousness associated with this level below that of the human. There seems to be a degree of autonomy on this level which is not found in the inorganic.

With man, experience becomes cumulative through the medium of language and culture generally. Human experience is social as well as individual, embedded in the accumulation of symbols, instruments, technologies, institutions, records, the arts, etc. Its complexity is also enormously enhanced by the fact of participation. Communication, participation and tools provide the basis for ideas and abstract thought eventuating in the sciences, philosophy and religion, as well as technologies.

We do not have to go outside nature and experience themselves to account for their manifold manifestations. Evolution, life, mind and consciousness, reflective thought and the arts are the natural outcomes of natural processes. Life, mind, meaning, consciousness and reflective thought are not different orders of existence from the rest of nature. They are rather qualities of behavior associated with organic life, possessing certain characteristics, and certain forms of organization.

There is thus continuity of organization and behavior from the simple components of the atom through the colloids and protein molecules, vegetable and animal life, to the most complex forms of art, science, philosophy, religion and other social institutions. Each level possesses the qualities of the levels below along with its own emergent characteristics. Man is a physical body and a biological organism as well as a creature of art, technology and reflective thought.

The significance of this interaction is that it precludes dualistic interpretations, because they explain nothing. Matter and mind are not different kinds of substances; they are, rather, different orders of events, even though associated with each other. The principles of association, individuality, organization, emergence and continuity are adequate to account for all the phenomena of nature and experience in "natural" terms without having to introduce discontinuities, dualisms, or the occult.

Philosophers have been classified in their general character as monist, dualist or pluralist. The monists were more sensitive to continuities and similarities throughout nature. The pluralists were more sensitive to distinctions, individualisms, discretenesses. Dewey's philosophy falls into none of these categories; if it were not a barbarism and a contradiction in terms, the label might be "pluralistic monism." Although Dewey disposed outright of dualism, he learned the lesson of both monists and pluralists. He was aware of individualities, of uniqueness and novelty, of distinction and variety. But his principle of association only enriched these perceptions. He saw the world as both organized and continuous, and as varied, creative, individualized.

THEORY OF KNOWLEDGE AND VALUATION. The world is both precarious and stable. Experience is both continuous and discontinuous; it is settled, regular and ordered in some aspects, and confused, uncertain and problematic in others. Life is a constant process in which the organism falls out of equilibrium with its environment and restores it. This is the essence of life.

But the restoration of equilibrium, the clarification of the confused, the solution of the problem are not automatic. This is the work of reflective thinking. We stop to think when we are in trouble. Troubles may vary from losing one's way to meeting a financial situation, developing a national policy, working out an artistic problem, or developing a new field in mathematics. Thus, ideas and thinking are instrumental in function. The fact that some men enjoy thinking for its own delight, in no way affects this instrumental function.

Dewey dismissed the general problem of knowledge as unreal because, whatever the differences in theories of knowledge, they are all based upon the common, but false, assumption that mind and matter are entirely disparate orders of existence. As Dewey saw it, the problem of knowledge is two-fold. On the one hand, it is always concrete and particular: how to know most effectively in a particular difficulty. On the other hand, there is the general problem of perfecting methods of inquiry.

The problem of knowledge is one with the problem of using the method of intelligence. The sciences embody the most disciplined expression of this method. Although the specific procedures of inquiry vary greatly from problem to problem, there is nonetheless a general pattern of method. There has been considerable argument among scientists and others whether there is *a* "scientific method" in view of the great variety of procedures exhibited in actual inquiries. The confusion is over the meaning of "method." If by "method" we mean temporal steps or procedures, then certainly there are as many methods as there are inquiries. Each has its own unique approach. If by "method" we mean necessary general characteristics of inquiry, then certainly there is a general method, not only of the sciences but of intelligence generally.

Dewey discussed these general phases of thinking many times. First there must be a problem. Next the problem must be located and defined; however, this "next" step is not to be taken as step number two from which one moves on to step number three. On the contrary, it should be seen as a phase of inquiry which, in fact, may not be completed until shortly before the final conclusion. Once one has clearly discerned the nature of his problem, the solution often becomes relatively simple; therefore these are phases of inquiry rather than temporal steps. Other phases are the ascertainment of the facts relevant to the problem, the formulation of hypotheses or ideas, reflection upon these in terms of the data, and finally conclusion and empirical test. The point to be emphasized is that the entire process is empirical, arising out of a difficulty in experience, dealing with data of experience and finally being tested in experience.

In *Logic: The Theory of Inquiry* Dewey argued that the forms of logic themselves are the product of experience in inquiry, and hence logic is a progressive discipline. He compared the improvement of scientific method in inquiry with the improvements in the art of metallurgy. In neither are there external canons or norms which must be met. These, rather, are generated in the pursuit of the art, whether metallurgy or inquiry. Hence, he considered logic as empirical as physics or biology, and insisted that the art of inquiry would continue to improve as did the other arts. The object of inquiry is what he called "warranted assertion," warranted because of the method employed, including empirical test.

One might reasonably assert that the problem of knowledge, method of inquiry and intelligence was the focal interest of Dewey. Certainly, this theme bulked large in his writings from the late nineteenth century up to the middle of the twentieth. His most compact work was the *Logic* published in his seventy-ninth year, and in his ninetieth year he and A. F. Bentley published *Knowing and the Known*.

There are two reasons for this continuining interest in knowledge and the method of inquiry. He doubtless felt that this problem was the strategic problem for philosophy in its technical aspects. Until the Cartesian dualism of mind and matter—along with the problem of knowledge it raised—was resolved, philosophic thought would be frustrated in dealing with the more human aspects of philosophy because this dualism was the citadel of classicism and the class society. The second reason is closely allied to the first. Until intelligence could be seen as the method for dealing with the problems and confusions of life and culture, and until intelligence was seen as instrumental to humane ends, civilization, and democracy in particular, would be in peril. Thus, while his interest in intelligence and inquiry was certainly very great, I think it could be argued that this interest was instrumental to his social-moral concerns.

Kant had argued that theoretical reason, that is, the sciences and reflective thinking generally, could tell us only of the facts of existence, but could tell us nothing of what ought to be. According to theoretical reason, nature—including human nature—was mechanistically determined, and had no place for freedom, duty, immortality or God. The moral and religious life could find no ground in existence as revealed by scientific inquiry. Thus, there was an impassable gulf between the "is" and the "ought" which could be bridged only by what he called practical reason, i.e., by faith.

For Dewey, Kant's argument posed a major problem: democracy as a way of life governed by shared interests, knowledge and communication, had a fatal flaw if men could not find norms of conduct by means of their intelligence, including the method of science. If principles and norms of conduct were not open to inquiry as were other matters, then men were at the mercy of external standards over which they had no control. Moreover,

Dewey was convinced that norms and principles of conduct had evolved in the same way as canons and norms of logic or metallurgy, jurisprudence or agriculture. Hence, the relation of inquiry to valuation was a crucial moral and social problem; it was the key to the problem of democracy and ethics. He says:

The problem of restoring integration and co-operation between man's beliefs about the world in which he lives and his beliefs about values and purposes that should direct his conduct is the deepest problem of modern life. It is the problem of any philosophy that is not isolated from that life.[11]

The problem of conduct is how to distinguish the preferable from the preferred, the satisfactory from the satisfying, the desirable from the desired. In their immediate form, there can be no comparison of values or desires. Each is just what it is, incomparable. But desires outrun possibilities. Selection must be made. Must we turn to some external standard such as the laws of Moses, or can experience generate its own criteria? As stated, desires and preferences in their immediate form reveal nothing of their comparative "worth." However, they do have consequences for other values we hold. One may ask how, then, we evaluate these other values. The situation here is much like that which a scientist meets. He does not question the great corpus of science, though he may raise a question about some particular item. He doubts only what in that situation is doubtful. He takes as settled what is not called into doubt, and uses that as instrumental in his inquiry.

So, in a value situation, we question only what in that situation is questionable. The great body of values may be undisturbed. There is no certainty or absolute finality. We make the best appraisal we can with the resources at our command and rectify it when it needs rectification.

Evaluation raises the question of the consequences of pursuing one particular desire. The problem of life is how to maximize satisfactions, which means making the most effective use of the resources at our disposal in the promotion of our whole kingdom of ends. We inherit at any time a tradition of principles and ideals. These we employ as reference points in evaluating consequences and costs. But principles and ideals themselves may be called into question and require reconstruction or abandonment. Thus, our value consciousness grows and evolves as does the culture generally.

Moreover, what we know about ourselves, our world, and particularly our culture, affects our ideals and principles. Dewey throughout his writings emphasizes the human significance of the sciences. He deplores the separation of the "natural" from the "human" sciences, for he believes that the natural sciences, when seen in their human context, are as human as any, and open up new possibilities for good and ill.

To understand that man is both a social and an individual creature makes a difference in our ideals and our moral principles. To see that men are members of communities with which their fortunes are bound up, rather than separate individuals, means a revolution in moral theory. To discern that our greatest good is to be found in shared experience provides us with an entirely different conception of an ideal life. To see the continuity of the old and the new, and the ever-present need to reconstruct both in order to effect continuity, saves us from the rut of the routineer as well as from the impatience and violence of the revolutionary. To recognize growth and creativity as the supreme condition for the enhancement of value is to open new vistas of human possibilities. In all Dewey's writings, one gets this sense that his ultimate concern is with the unlimited expansion of the possibilities of human life.

The nature of the moral situation, then, is to make choices and decisions that will maximize the values of the situation for all concerned. Making such choices and decisions requires the method of intelligence, of the sciences, and the fruits of the sciences.

MAN AND CULTURE. Markedly influenced by James' *Psychology*, Dewey departed even further from the psychological tradition. Dewey never lost sight of the fact that man is a biological organism, however much more he is. Man's biological character was the basis from which his human character emerged. Not to do justice to his continuity with the biological world is to overlook the very sources of his being and, at the same time, his distinctively human traits.

Dewey's conception of the continuous interaction of organism and environment plays a fundamental role in his psychological and social theory. We cannot speak of man as a phenomenon separate from his cultural environment.

The individual enters life as a helpless infant and from the beginning is dependent upon those about him. As he interacts with his social environment, he must accommodate himself to that environment in order to control his relations with it. In that accommodation, the human environment begins to shape his character. However, he does not passively assume the design of the social mold. As an active organism with a distinctive organic constitution, with biases and preferences, he modifies his environment to suit his distinctive needs. His character is the cumulative product of his interaction with his environment, which for him is essentially social.

Dewey's emphasis upon the continuity of man with his biological heritage and with his social environment was a clear departure from the tradition.

The interaction of human beings, namely, association, is not different in origin from other modes of interaction. There is a peculiar absurdity in the question of how individuals become social, if the question is taken literally. . . . Everything that exists in as far as it is known and knowable is in interaction with other things. It is associated, as well as solitary, single. . . . Significance resides not in the bare fact of association, therefore, but in the consequences that flow from the distinctive patterns of human association. . . . The significant consideration is that assemblage of organic human beings transforms sequence and coexistence into participation.[12]

At the time Dewey wrote *Human Nature and Conduct,* the heredity-environment controversy was at its height. It is reasonable to assume that this book had much to do with bringing it to a close. While he made clear the influence of the social environment upon the self, he was always aware that selves are also biological organisms. However, he saw that the hereditarians had misconceived the nature of biological heredity. They had taken for granted that man, like the lower animals, inherited specific behavior patterns, i.e., instincts. The existence of language and tools, however, signifies a very different kind of heredity. Man inherits the capacity to learn—to learn from others and to learn for himself—to make and use tools, to create culture.

From these two distinctive characteristics of human nature—language and the capacity to make and use tools—man developed the third: culture building. Human evolution is no longer merely a matter of chance evolutionary accidents but is now in large measure cultural. To the extent that man can understand himself and his culture, and bring both under the control of an ethical intelligence, he assumes control of his own destiny and directs his own evolutionary process.

SOCIO-MORAL PHILOSOPHY. The socio-moral emphasis dominates all of Dewey's writings. His metaphysics, theory of knowledge, concept of man and culture and his aesthetics all provide the necessary foundation for his social and moral theory. "Social" and "moral" are joined here because in this way they reflect Dewey's concept of the inseparability of organism and environment.

Democracy was his dominant ideal—"ideal" precisely because it is the way of life most congenial to the nature of man and because the traits of the democratic community are those which make for greater effectiveness of both communities and their individual members. It is the way of life which is necessary to "the best, the richest and fullest experience possible" for men, and nothing less is good enough. It provides the necessary conditions for human nature to exhibit its distinctive and superlative possibilities.

In the first place, democracy is a shared, co-operative life in which the individual and the social are mutually complementary aspects of behavior. Varied and often conflicting individual interests are synthesized into more complex common purposes which relate the individual interests to one another organically. Democracy calls forth thought, imagination, and intelligence, and gives them the fullest opportunity of expression; at the same time, these qualities are essential to the democratic process. For this reason, the problem of knowledge and the nature of intelligence loomed large in all of Dewey's thinking. The perfecting of democracy and of the method of intelligence are interdependent, if not indeed synonymous, particularly when we consider the extension of the latter to the whole community.

Democracy is also the necessary condition for continued growth and creativity. One might say that growth-creativity for all men is Dewey's "ultimate" ideal and that democracy is the necessary condition for its realization. Dewey was always wary about "ultimate" ideals because of their abstractness and their remoteness from the concrete problems of life. They tend to harden the intellectual and moral arteries by their fixity. However growth and democracy may reasonably be designated as ultimate in the sense that they are comprehensive and inclusive of his other ideals for men.

The terms "growth" and "creativity" should caution us against any development that puts an end to growing. They remind us that life is organic and a continuing process, that each day, each epoch makes its own peculiar demands upon life. The ideal of growth requires that our varied interests and purposes and our more specific ideals form an organic synthesis in which each tends to maintain, support and promote the other, thus achieving integrity of character.

Means and ends are a continuous process with no final ending. To conceive an end is to conceive the process of which it is a member. Concern for ends is concern for a more comprehensive and far-sighted view of the process; no step is means only or ends only. The assessment of means-ends, therefore, must take into account the total situation. What are the central realities out of which the ends of democracy or growth are to be realized? A first and important fact is that men generally, but in America in particular, have glimpsed democracy. They have experienced democratic relations or qualities in their own lives or have heard of it in others.

A second reality is the rise of science and its offspring, technology. These have had a most profound effect upon the modern world; their effects are indeed without number. They have altered the environment in which every institution functions and in so doing have subjected them to severe strains. "The combined effect of science and technology has released more productive energies in a bare hundred years than stands to the credit of prior human history in its entirety." [13]

"Thanks to science and technology we now live in an age of

potential plenty. . . . The habits of desire and effort that were
bred in the age of scarcity do not readily subordinate themselves
and take the place of the matter-of-course routine that becomes
appropriate to them when machines and impersonal power
have the capacity to liberate man from bondage to the strivings
that were once needed to make secure his physical basis." [14]

Although we live in the prospect of plenty, and security is a
matter of fact for most men, we still emphasize the need for the
incentives springing from insecurity to move men to productive
work. The fact is, of course, that for many of those who are
secure, incentives are intrinsic to productive work. The joys of
achievement move men to much greater effort than ever did
the scourge of insecurity.

Although science and technology have profoundly changed
the basic structures and relations of life, we still have little
common understanding of the significance of that change. Old
ideas, customs, modes of thought and values have been rendered
archaic. We think in terms of an individualism that may have
had relevance on the frontier but which has no relevance in the
highly corporate civil collective society that we now are.

What means, then, are appropriate to our particular circumstances? The means appropriate to further extend democracy
and to remedy our specific ills are intrinsic to our end, which
is growth. First among these is of course the educational task.
Fundamentally, it is two-fold: on the one hand there is need to
make the method of intelligence, that is the method of the
sciences, a general competence which is used not only in
technical matters but in matters of human relations as well.
Moral education is really education in perfecting the processes
of deliberation, or more simply, the method of intelligence
applied in moral matters, both individual and social.

A second function of education is that of cultivating the arts of
social action, of learning how to engage in co-operative or shared
activity with effectiveness. This means the shaping of habit and
disposition requisite to a democratic society.

Education in its broadest sense is the work of the culture. This
means that every institution and practice should be examined
for its educative consequences and reconstructed in terms of
educative ends. The human consequences of any institution are
of even greater significance than its more obvious and immediate

ends. A good society is one in which every institution and activity is judged by its effects upon human character.

Dewey was highly skeptical of all wholesale solutions such as capitalism, socialism, communism, to say nothing of fascism. These he saw as general nostrums which ignored the specific requirements of specific conditions. Although he was sympathetic to socialism because of its more humane ends, nonetheless he rejected it. The reason is simple: the only method he could see as a continuing progressive method was that of scientific intelligence.

AESTHETIC THEORY. Dewey envisioned a culture in which all activities would possess as much as possible the quality of the artistic-aesthetic, as they now may do for most professional people, scientists, medical men, lawyers, educators, managers. This quality should become universal because it is both a means and an end of human life. In art the instrumental and the consummatory coalesce. Each stage of the activity is both preparatory and consummatory. It is a consummation of what has gone before and a preparation for what is to follow. Dewey greatly expanded the common usage of the term "art": any activity carried on with loving care for its outcome is by definition art.

The narrower usage of art as confined to the "fine arts" is, he argued, a result of dualism of thought and action, activity and receptivity, means and ends, the instrumental and the consummatory. "The limiting terms that define art are routine at one extreme and capricious impulse at the other." [15]

Any activity that is productive of objects whose perception is an immediate good and whose operation is a continual source of enjoyable perception of other events exhibits fineness of art.[16]

A genuinely aesthetic object is not exclusively consummatory but is causally productive as well. A consummatory object that is not also instrumental turns in time to the dust and ashes of boredom. The "eternal" quality of great art is its renewed instrumentality for further consummatory experiences.[17]

In an artistic-aesthetic experience there is a coalescence of means and ends. Causal conditions are seen *as means* to a desired consequence, and hence continuous with it.

The connection of means-consequences is never one of bare succession in time, such that the element that is means is past and gone when the end is instituted. An active process is strung out temporarily, but there is a deposit at each stage and point entering cumulatively and constitutively into the outcome. A genuine instrumentality *for* is always an organ *of* an end. It confers continued efficacy upon the object in which it is embodied.[18]

It is this cumulative quality which characterizes art. The work has purpose and intent from the beginning and is cumulatively consummatory.

Dewey distinguished between the artistic and the aesthetic, though they are indissoluble. The term "artistic" characterizes the production of an art object. The term "aesthetic" characterizes the receptive phase of enjoyment. But the production is itself governed by the aesthetic response of the artist, and the one enjoying the object must himself create a "work of art." That is, he too must engage in an active phase. Perception is outgoing and constructive as well as receptive. Thus the "art object" is the external physical object, the result of the work of the artist. The "work of art" is the work of the perceiver, as well as of the artist.

Dewey began his discussion in *Art as Experience* with his chapter on "The Live Creature" in which he discussed the equilibrative relations of the live creature with his environment. In a later chapter on "Having an Experience" he discussed the ideal of this equilibrative process. In this chapter he describes the artistic-aesthetic experience in its generic character.

. . . we have *an* experience when the material experienced runs its course to fulfillment. Then and then only is it integrated within and demarcated in the general stream of experience from other experiences. A piece of work is finished in a way that is satisfactory; a problem receives its solution; a game is played through; a situation, whether that of eating a meal, playing a game of chess, carrying on a conversation, writing a book, or taking part in a political campaign, is so rounded out that its close is a consummation and not a cessation. Such an experience is a whole and carries with it its own individualizing quality and self-sufficiency. It is *an* experience.[19]

Thus we see that there is no sharp division between the artistic-aesthetic and the intellectual or the practical. The distinction is that an aesthetic experience is its own justification. But the intellectual or the practical, though distinctively instrumental in character, may also possess an aesthetic-artistic quality when incentive is internal to the activity. One objection to Dewey's instrumentalism has been that thinking should be its own end because men can find it intrinsically delightful. This objection does not touch the substance of instrumentalism, for instrumentalism is a theory of the function of thought or of art; each has consequences and is to be judged by its consequences. The appropriateness of any act is determined by how well it performs its function, not by the fact of enjoyment or lack of it.

So for Dewey the artistic-aesthetic is the highest consummation of experience and nature. It is the ideal quality of experience because of *both* its consummatory and its instrumental quality. Morals at their best are really aesthetic-artistic in character, as is religion. A moral situation is one in which desires, ends, ideals, purposes are in conflict. In the process of deliberation each factor in conflict plays itself out in imagination in order that its consequences may be envisioned. Decision is just and reasonable to the degree that each factor has had a fair hearing, has told its full story and been taken into account. A decision which maximizes the values possible in that situation is as much a work of art as is a picture or a monument.

The religious experience as a unified coherent perspective on existence is of the same quality. One might say that it is the superlative of the artistic-aesthetic because it embraces the widest possible range and variety of materials and of values. It is the work of consummate imagination and intelligence.

Since Dewey considered the moral and the communicative the great instrumental functions of art, I close this discussion with his own words:

Relief from continuous moral activity—in the conventional sense of moral—is itself a moral necessity. The service of art and play is to engage and release impulses in ways quite different from those in which they are occupied and employed in ordinary activities . . . their spontaneity and liberation from external necessities permits to them an enhancement and vitality of meaning not possible in preoccupation with immediate needs. . . . In saying then that art and play have a moral office . . . it is asserted that they are responsible to life, to the enriching and freeing of its meanings, not that they are responsible to a moral code, commandment or special task.[20]

Because the objects of art are expressive, they communicate. I do not say that communication to others is the intent of an artist. But it is the consequence of his work—which indeed lives only in communication when it operates in the experience of others. . . . In the end, works of art are the only media of complete and unhindered communication between man and man that can occur in a world full of gulfs and walls that limit community of experience.[21]

EDUCATION. I have intentionally left the discussion of education to the end. In a sense Dewey's theory of education is the capstone of his philosophy; in education his ideas come to a focus and get their test. However, one who has read only his educational writings can have but a slender grasp of his educational philosophy, for it is bound up with his whole thought. Moreover, if we identify education with all the agencies that shape and form character, it is clear that education is man's chief instrument for social and moral progress.

Dewey's philosophy is a perception of our civilization's intrinsic possibilities of assimilating advanced science and technology to the ends of democracy—that is, to human life and growth. An education that would be the great instrument in that task must be informed and inspired by such a philosophy. Inasmuch as we have not yet shed the intellectual and moral habits of a pre-industrial, pre-scientific, and pre-democratic culture, his philosophy is revolutionary. It is so because he purges the archaic forms of thought and disposition.

We should note that his great work on education was titled *Democracy and Education*—in other words, not just any education, but the particular education which would shape the understanding, dispositions and character necessary to a democracy. If Dewey has had influence it is because there is much that is democractic in our culture and his thought has helped to clarify and implement social and educational thought. If he has been misunderstood, or but partially understood, it is because there is so much in our thinking and feeling that is still pre-democratic and pre-scientific. Our common sense is encumbered with hangovers of an earlier civilization.

Dewey would have us study education in its informal as well as its formal aspects, because in the former it is most effective and pervasive. He has remarked that education is life; indeed, it is the very essence of human life and culture. The continuity of human culture depends upon communication of thought, feeling, habits, skills, ideals and understandings from generation to generation. The newborn child is only a human animal; he has to learn to become a human being. Without doubt his most complex task is among his earliest—learning language. Here we see learning processes at their best: there is involvement with others in shared purposeful activities, a sense of genuine problem, intense interest and concentration in the thoughtful effort to solve the problem, a search for meanings, an effort to communicate by gesture or speech, and an experimental trying out of varied lines of thought and action until the problem is solved and the activity effectively executed. This is in germ the substance of learning method; good teaching is simply the provision of opportunity and the creation of need for the learner to engage in the method of learning.

Learning is modification of behavior; it might occur in development of skills, changing of attitudes, developing new purposes and interests, acquiring new tastes, clarifying and expanding understandings, clarification of confusions, surmounting of obstacles and difficulties, resolution of problems. But not every activity is educative. Just as the routine and the capricious mark the extreme limits of the artistic-esthetic, so do they mark the limits within which learning occurs. Between these extremes we find interest and purpose, without which there is no meaningful learning.

Because man is an essentially social creature, meaningful learning is a function of participation, of a social situation in which interest and purpose are shared. It could scarcely be otherwise since activities are social. Even though a person may study a problem by himself, the social character of the problem is not altered for it arises in a social matrix. In fact, individualization is itself a function of socialization; it is defining for one's self one's unique and peculiar role in varied social relations.

Learning is growth of experience in meaning, in perception of the connections among things and processes. It is through the growth of meaning that the child increases his control, and growth of meaning comes largely by way of communication. Formal education has apparently relied primarily on communication for its medium. I say "apparently" because what is often found in formal education is a truncated communication. Communication is at least a two-way matter, an affair of participation, of common purpose. Printed matter and speech are not of necessity communicative. Communication is a function of community, and community involves common experience and common concerns, common activities.

We have referred to the arts as the supreme communicative medium. While the esthetic experience is its own end, it is not without its consequences for feeling, disposition, attitude. It is for this reason that the arts are also the supreme educative medium. There could be no more severe criticism of the formal education of the past than to note the anesthetic character of the school environment and educative materials such as textbooks, nor is there anything more hopeful about present trends than the improved esthetic quality of the school environment and school materials. Yet we have much further to go. This is not to say that the study of art should become the major concern of the schools, but rather that the atmosphere and spirit of all the school's activities should take on a more artistic-esthetic quality.

Activities should not only be shared and purposeful; they also should be thoughtful, experimental. For thinking is the method of noting the relation between what we do and the results, between our ideas and their consequences. Thus all genuine thinking is experimental.

Thinking *is* the method of intelligent learning, of learning that employs and rewards mind. We speak, legitimately enough, about the method of thinking, but the important thing to bear in mind about method is that thinking is method, the method of intelligent experience in the course which it takes.[22]

Thinking is thus equivalent to an explicit rendering of the intelligent element in our experience. It makes it possible to act with an end in view. It is the condition of our having aims.[23]

Thinking, in other words, is the intentional endeavor to discover *specific* connections between something which we do and the consequences which result, so that the two become continuous.[24]

We have spoken of the method of learning. What about the method of teaching? In general, we can say that teaching method, like learning method, must be thoughtful, experimental. The task of the teacher is to see that the conditions essential to learning are present. The teacher's problem is to insure that learning is progressive—that is, cumulative, and that it amounts to something in terms of the possibilities of continued growth. As the representative of the culture it is his function to provide the materials of that culture which will most enrich any learning situation and at the same time keep experience flexible, integral and growing.

The problem of subject-matter is closely related to that of method. As a matter of fact, a learning experience involves both the "what" and the "how" of learning. In general terms we may say that the subject-matter of education is those selected materials of the culture which offer most promise for the continued growth of experience in meaning and control. Among these, the resources of communication—including languages, mathematics and some art form—are of supreme importance. Closely following is a *working* understanding of human nature and the attitudes and skills involved in associated life. These are the fundamentals.

To carry our own weight and assume our responsibilities we require competence in a chosen occupation and in our domestic and civic occupations. If we conceive of a culture as a vast complex of occupations and specializations, we must say that education in a culture requires familiarity with the occupational aspects and relationships of that culture. For competent citizenship and at the same time for personal development, it is necessary to understand our world in its geographic, historic, ethnic and economic aspects. Nor is the world of literature and the arts a merely personal ornament and enjoyment. It is the medium through which we take on the most refined and highly developed values of the culture. Far from slighting subject-matter, the teacher has to have a vastly wider grasp of subject-matter in order to supply those materials which are psychologically most relevant and which at the same time prepare for ever wider and growing experience. But such subject-matters can not be prescribed in advance, certainly not in the earlier stages of learning. Subject-matter is integral with method, and the teacher, like the doctor, must prescribe what is of most importance to the situation.

It was unfortunate, I believe, that Dewey in his discussion of the aims of education remarked that education as such has no aims; only parents, teachers, and others—not an abstract idea like education—have aims. Although his whole discussion of aims in education is quite consistent with his general point of view, it has led many people to assume that he advocated no direction in education, that children were to do what they pleased and that his pedagogy was soft.

The opposite is true. No philosophy of education is more demanding of both teachers and students than his. The point he wished to emphasize was that the aims of education must be intrinsic to the process. Obviously Dewey had some aims for education, and he might have avoided some misunderstanding if he had formulated these explicitly.

His all-encompassing aim for education was growth, continuing growth. So he said of education that it had no end save more education. Elsewhere he says that there is no end to growth other than growth itself. In short, he equated education and growth. Here as elsewhere we find his means and ends continuous, the means implicit in the ends. To cite some of his means we might refer to participation, communication, thinking, art, purposeful activity. These, then, are both means and ends, though there is no external end to any of them.

In another sense, we might say that his aim for education was the shaping of habits, dispositions and modes of thought and feelings which are essential to a democratic society. Education was for him both means and end, the primary instrument of democracy. One might equally say that the democratic method, the method of intelligence and education were synonymous. To repeat, for him, a democratic education was the *only* means by which a democratic society might assimilate an advanced science and technology to its own ends, that is, to humane needs and purposes.

CONCLUSION. We have considered several aspects of Dewey's thinking in order to illustrate how he expressed the genius of American civilization and at the same time expressed a genius of his own. To the genius of the civilization which he inherited, he contributed insights by means of which America might mobilize its human and democratic resources to bring all activities under the control of human ends.

FIVE

Soviet Attitudes

Toward John Dewey as an Educator

William W. Brickman

INTRODUCTION. The educational ideas and activities of John Dewey have become familiar to educators all around the globe. That many of them have shown great interest in him is evidenced by the large number of discussions and translations of his writings in numerous languages.[1] The resultant reputation of Dewey in foreign countries has managed to persist in spite of downgrading criticism in certain circles in the United States.

Only in one part of the world, behind the Iron Curtain, does Dewey seem to have encountered serious hostility, not because of intrinsic philosophical or methodological considerations but rather because of opposition to his political views and activities. Dewey has become *persona non grata* wherever the ideology of communism is predominant. In some Communist areas he has been ignored; in others, bitterly attacked. Poland is the only Communist country which has issued anything of a pro-Dewey nature—a recent translation of *How We Think*.[2]

The country which has reacted with vehemence and venom toward Dewey is the Soviet Union. For some three decades his name has been anathema in Soviet educational circles. Yet, until 1930 or so, many Soviet educators showed enthusiasm for his ideas and work. It is pertinent to inquire about the reasons for this radical change in attitude. It is interesting, at the same time, to go back into an earlier period and to trace the history of Dewey's educational reputation in Russia and in the Union of Soviet Socialist Republics.[3]

RUSSIAN-AMERICAN CULTURAL AND EDUCATIONAL RELA-
TIONS. First-hand American knowledge of Russian life and

society apparently began with the account written by John Quincy Adams, who served as secretary in 1781–1783 to Francis Dana, the first United States diplomatic representative to the court of Catherine the Great. All through the nineteenth century, American diplomats, travelers, and teachers published reports on Russian life, culture, and education.[4] The newly established U. S. Bureau of Information contributed information on Russian schools starting in 1875, probably because of the impact of the first Commissioner, Henry Barnard, who had in 1855 included a short contribution on Russia in the first volume of his *American Journal of Education*. As the Americans showed an interest in Russia, so did the Russians in the new republic. Such nineteenth century intellectuals as Alexander Hertsen and others looked to the United States as the model of a democratic society in which there was remarkable material progress. The liberals were sympathetic to America because of the liberation of the Negroes, the opposition to Tsarist tyranny, and the writings of Mark Twain and later of Jack London. To some extent, America became less popular in radical Russian circles from the post-Civil War period until the end of the century, due to the rise of Marxism which pointed to the evils of industrial capitalism.

Probably the high point of Russian educational prestige in America was the decade or two following the Philadelphia Centennial Exposition of 1876. Admiration for the exhibit of the work of the Imperial Technical School of Moscow by President John D. Runkle of the Massachusetts Institute of Technology and by Dean Calvin M. Woodward of the engineering school of Washington University led to the adoption of these methods by many American schools.[5] By way of historical reciprocation, Russian educators, including Rector Albert P. Pinkevich of the Second Moscow State University, came to the University of Cincinnati to learn directly from President Herman Schneider the details of the co-operative theoretical-practical program he had initiated in 1906 when he was dean of the college of engineering. The report by Pinkevich credited Schneider with originating a program "combining theoretical study with practical work,"[6] a concept very popular in the contemporary Soviet Union.

It is not difficult to demonstrate mutual interest involving the

United States and the U. S. S. R. from the time of the revolution of 1917 onward. It is enough to be aware that the relationship of John Dewey to Russia had a multi-faceted historical context.

MODERN EDUCATION IN RUSSIA. Before the history of the Russians' knowledge about Dewey can be explored, it will be first necessary to review another type of context—Russian familiarity with the world of educational ideas of which Dewey's educational theory was a part.

During the seventeenth century, the Russian intellectual leaders may have been familiar with the ideas of Jan Amos Comenius (Komensky), or at least with his name. There was definite Russian knowledge in the eighteenth century of the educational thought of Michel de Montaigne, John Locke, Denis Diderot, and of Jean Jacques Rousseau. In point of fact, Catherine the Great received from Diderot in 1776 a "Plan d'une Université pour la Russie."[7] In the nineteenth century, Russian educational thinkers knew the work and ideas of Johann Heinrich Pestalozzi, Philipp Emanuel von Fellenberg, Johann Friedrich Herbart, and Friedrich Froebel.

Konstantin D. Ushinskii (1824–70) wrote a description of education in the United States, even though he never had the opportunity of seeing American schools. Count Leo N. Tolstoi visited the schools of France, Germany, Italy, and Switzerland, and knew European educational literature. In an essay published in his educational journal, *Yasnaya Polyana,* Tolstoi discussed briefly the method of geography teaching as presented in Peter Parley's textbook, which he knew from the 1837 translation.[8] At his school, which he opened in 1857 on his country estate at Yasnaya Polyana, Tolstoi gave instruction without cost to peasant children, allowed pupils freedom to choose their studies, encouraged equality of teachers and pupils, and dispensed with external discipline as well as with textbooks and formal lessons.

It was the international fame of Tolstoi as a novelist, thinker, and social reformer that probably directed Jane Addams in 1896 to Yasnaya Polyana. The Russian reformer gave Miss Addams $250 from the royalties of *Resurrection* for Hull House.[9] Another important American visitor was President William

Rainey Harper of the University of Chicago, who journeyed to Tolstoi's home in 1900.[10] From these meetings was forged a strong link between Russia and Chicago. Russians like Prince Kropotkin, a guest at Hull House in 1899, and those who attended the St. Louis Exposition of 1904, had opportunities to appreciate the sociological and intellectual significance of Chicago at that time.

The basis for an understanding and acceptance of John Dewey's ideas on education is evident from the fact that the Russians were acquainted with and used the modern and progressive pedagogical practices which were the heritage of several centuries of education in Europe. The theories and practices proposed by Dewey, while not consciously derived from nineteenth century pedagogy, had much in common with those of the European educators. To those educational leaders already cited, at least one more of Russian birth and training might be added: Konstantin N. Ventsel (Wentzel), born in 1857, who propounded Progressivism in education before and after the Russian Revolution.[11] I have not been able to determine whether there was any connection between Dewey and Ventsel, but one does appear to have been possible.

DEWEY'S IDEAS IN TSARIST RUSSIA. It would be interesting to know precisely when Dewey's educational ideas first became known to Russian educators. There is a possibility that Alexander Zelenko, a Russian engineer who stayed at Hull House during 1903–4, carried information about Dewey's work when he returned to Moscow in 1904.[12] It will be recalled that John Dewey served as chairman of the department of philosophy, psychology, and pedagogy at the University of Chicago from 1894 to 1904. Between 1896 and 1903, he directed the Laboratory School at the University of Chicago. Among his works on education during this period were *Interest as Related to Will* (1896), *My Pedagogic Creed* (1897), *Ethical Principles Underlying Education* (1897), *The School and Society* (1899), and *The Child and the Curriculum* (1902).

However, alert Russian pedagogues might have learned about Dewey independently through his books—translations such as the Czech rendering of *The School and Society* in 1904, and Lucinda P. Boggs' German dissertation on the application of Dewey's theory of interest to education (University of Halle, 1901).[13] As in the case of Ventsel, the problem of the origin of Russian interest in Dewey requires further research in documents which would be difficult to locate today in Russia.

The complete chain of events whereby Dewey's ideas began to penetrate Russia is still to be established by documentary research. It is likely that Alexander Zelenko became exposed to Dewey's viewpoint during his residence at Hull House in 1903–4. As Jane Dewey points out, the Deweys were "regular visitors" to Hull House and "formed warm personal friendships with its residents, especially with Jane Addams."[14] John Dewey became a member of the board of trustees of Hull House and lectured there on social psychology.[15] "Dewey's faith in democracy as a guiding force in education took on both a sharper and deeper meaning because of Hull House and Jane Addams."[16]

Zelenko returned in 1904 to Russia and apparently took with him not only the idea of settlement work as practiced at Hull House, but also Deweyan ideas on education. The first Russian educators who accepted Dewey through the intermediacy of Zelenko were Stanislav T. Shatskii and Louise Shleger.[17] Shatskii had turned from music and prepared himself, under the influence of Tolstoi's example, to help the poor peasant and the poor urban dweller. In the words of Shatskii himself, "In 1904 new educational principles coming from American settlements, penetrated into Moscow. These principles were based upon the idea of social reform through education."[18] More specifically, Shatskii stated in an interview with the late Professor Thomas Woody around 1928, "Wrestling with methods in relation to children's interests and the possible development of their capacities, I drew greatest assistance from the careful analysis by John Dewey, being deeply impressed by his 'philosophy of pragmatism' which persistently demanded careful examination of theoretical ideas in their practical application."[19] This statement by Shatskii was in reference to the First Moscow Settlement, a group of children's clubs founded by Zelenko, Shleger, and Shatskii in 1906. A year before, Louise Shleger had established a kindergarten for fifteen children of poor workers at

Shelkovo, a suburb of Moscow. This settlement, which became in effect an experimental school, led to the arrest of Zelenko and Shatskii "for trying to plant socialism in the minds of little children," as well as to the closing of the school itself.[20] In 1908, the school was reopened. After the Revolution it was renamed the First Experimental Station on Public Education and was operated under the direction of Shatskii.

It is also worthy of note that the translation of one of Dewey's pedagogical works, *The School and Society*,[21] appeared in 1907, the year Shatskii's work was discontinued by orders of the Tsar. It may be, however, that Russian pedagogues also knew of Dewey's writings through translations and pedagogical works in other languages. Another publication of Dewey's writings prior to the Revolution was *Psychology and Pedagogical Thought* (*How We Think*) in 1915.[22]

Further research is necessary to establish any definite connections between Dewey and other pre-Revolutionary Russian educators. There are many similarities, for example, between Dewey and Pavel P. Blonskii, who was a pioneer in the *trudovaya shkola* (activity school) and later in pedology, or child study; M. M. Pistrak; and Nadezhda K. Krupskaya. It is reasonable to assume that they were at least acquainted with the Deweyan pedagogy prior to 1917.

THE EARLY REVOLUTIONARY PERIOD. The advent of the Revolution made it necessary to recast the educational system of Russia. Educators began looking in all directions, particularly toward the recognized educators of Europe—Ovide Decroly in Belgium and Georg Kerschensteiner in Germany, for example— for guidance as to the best methods of achieving a revolution in education in accordance with the spirit of communism. They borrowed freely in the early years "from Montessori to Kerschensteiner, from Dewey to Lay and to Decroly."[23] The Soviet Government issued translations of works on psychology and education in English, French and German.[24] Nadezhda K. Krupskaya, wife of Vladimir I. Lenin, and a highly influential educational leader, showed in her pedagogical writings that she was acquainted with the New School movement led by Cecil Reddie of England, Edmond Demolins of France, and Hermann Lietz of Germany, as well as with William James.[25] Truly, the early Soviet educators "scoured the world for educational ideas." [26]

The Soviet quest for foreign educational ideas and practices extended to the United States. "One of the first American pedagogical inventions to caress the Russian realm was the Dalton Laboratory Plan," which appealed to the Communist leaders of the Soviet Union mainly because "a pupil was made to work according to a plan."[27] The new pedagogical periodicals issued after the Revolution contained "many articles dealing with American educational theories and book reviews of works of American psychologists and educators." [28] Krupskaya, in particular, valued highly the work of some American educators. She recommended to Soviet educational workers the books of Dean Samuel Chester Parker of the University of Chicago, in spite of the fact that Parker's book which was especially singled out referred to the Russian Revolution as "a terrible farce and a tragedy foisted on an illiterate people." [29] It is also interesting to note that Parker regarded the writings and experiments of John Dewey, who "ranks very high among American professors of philosophy," as "the most influential factor in stimulating a general revision of educational theory in the United States." [30] According to an academic visitor to the Soviet Union in 1926, Scott Nearing, "Kilpatrick, Thorndike, Dewey and other American educators are almost as well known in the Soviet Union today as they are in the United States." [31] Mrs. Beatrice Ensor, founder of the New Era Fellowship in 1919, testified about 1927, "Dewey, Kilpatrick, Thorndike, Montessori, Decroly, Washburne, Parkhurst, are as well known in Soviet Russia as in their own countries." [32]

Lucy L. W. Wilson, a Philadephia high school principal who visited Soviet Russia in 1927, reported that Krupskaya "asked me about Dewey, Thorndike, Watson; projects, project curriculums, and Kilpatrick; individualized and group work, the Platoon, Dalton, and Winnetka plans; Bird Baldwin and preschool education; continuation schools. . . ." [33] It is clear that Krupskaya had much more than a superficial acquaintanceship with the theories and practices of education in the United States.

Interest in Dewey seemed to develop with the beginnings of

the new Soviet state. In 1918, only three years after its original publication, there appeared in Moscow a Russian translation of *Schools of Tomorrow* with a preface by the noted educator, I. I. Gorbunov-Posadov, who had edited the 1907 Russian translation of *The School and Society*.[34] During the following year, a second edition of *Psikhologiya i pedagogika mishleniya*[35] appeared, and in 1920 the second edition of *The School and Society* was published.[36]

It was not possible for me to obtain a full record of the Russian translations of Dewey's educational writings during the first decade of the Soviet regime, in spite of a search of the card catalogue of the Lenin Library in Moscow and the libraries of the pedagogical institutes and universities in the various cities of the U. S. S. R. What follows, therefore, is but a listing which possibly covers only a portion of the Russian translations of Dewey's works on education: *Introduction to Educational Philosophy*, apparently a 62-page extract from *Democracy and Education*, translated by Stanislav Shatskii, 1921;[37] the third edition of *Psychology and Pedagogical Thought*, 1922;[38] the second edition of *Schools of Tomorrow*, 1922;[39] the second edition of *The School and Society*, translated by Stanislav Shatskii, 1923;[40] *The School and the Child*, 1922 and 1923 editions;[41] and *The School and Society*,[42] translated by G. A. Luchinskii, 1924 and 1925. There does not seem to have been any Russian translation since the 1925 edition of *The School and Society*.[43]

It is clear that Dewey's ideas were well known in Soviet educational circles before his visit there in June, 1928. According to Anna Louise Strong, who apparently visited the U. S. S. R. in 1922 or 1923, the early Soviet educational reform "is modeled more on the Dewey ideas of education than on anything else we know in America. Every new book by Dewey is seized and eagerly translated into Russian for consultation. Then they make their own additions."[44] A visitor to the U. S. S. R. in 1926, Professor Samuel N. Harper of the University of Chicago, reported that "in my study of the schools I was helped by several older teachers, and particularly, by a Russian girl who had just returned from three years' study at Teachers College, Columbia, full of the ideas of Dewey, Counts, and Kilpatrick."[45]

I have attempted during three all-too-brief trips to the Soviet Union in 1957, 1958, and 1960, to locate monographs on John Dewey's educational thought and work. In an interview, September 9, 1958, at the Institute of the Theory and History of Pedagogy, Academy of Pedagogical Sciences of the R. S. F. S. R., in Moscow, Professor Vladimir A. Veikshan, a leading Soviet historian of education and comparative educationist, called attention to two monographs, one by "Komarovskova," published in 1926, and one by Shevkin, published in 1952. The latter will be described later in this essay. A consultation of the first edition of *Bolshaya Sovetskaya Entsiklopediya* at the Lenin Library disclosed the following bibliographical entry at the end of the article on "Dzhon Diyui": B. B. Komarovskii, "Filosofiya vospitaniya Dzhona Diyui v svyazi s istoriei amerikanskoi pedagogiki," Volume I, "Sovremennie pedagogicheskie techeniya" (Baku: 1930).[46] Unfortunately, the card catalogue did not include this work. Even the search by two library officials did not yield any record of Komarovskii's monograph. Interestingly, a copy of this book, the title of which means in English, "Contemporary Pedagogical Movements: Volume I, John Dewey's Educational Philosophy in Relation to the History of American Pedagogy," is available in the library of Teachers College, Columbia University. It is not likely, in view of the subsequent history of John Dewey's reputation in Russia, that more than a work or two of monographic proportions would have been written on the American educator's ideas.

The relationship of Shatskii to Dewey prior to and after the Revolution has already been outlined. It must not be assumed that the Russian was so full of Deweyism that, as in the case of many educators all over the world, he was blind to other forces. There is no doubt that he was thoroughly aware of the significance of the Russian Revolution for education. In his interview with Professor Thomas Woody, he said, "In 1917, my idea of labor education took a definite form, now in keeping with a new political insight, and influenced profoundly by Krupskaya and the works of Marx and Lenin, whom I number among my greatest teachers."[47] His new conviction led to membership in the Communist party in 1924.[48] In spite of his interest in Dewey, evidenced by his translations and other writings, Shatskii found that he could no longer adhere to the ideas of "free education" which were expressed by Tolstoi and Dewey. "Our outline and theories, many derived from abroad, had to be modified for transplanting to Russian soil." [49] The new Soviet society required an education which laid stress on the indoctrination of Communist dogmas which would contribute to the formation of a Communist mind. "The uniformity and order of a disciplined, collective society is better than the chaos and waste that are inevitable in a 'free' and individualistic one. To lay the educational bricks in building socialism is the high duty of current pedagogy. I wish to take part in this work till the end of life." [50] In other words, Shatskii became a loyal Communist, and he continued to make use of Deweyan and other Progressive educational practices toward the realization of a dogmatic aim which would be contrary to Dewey's thought.

Pavel P. Blonskii, like Shatskii, began with the pedagogical ideas of Tolstoi and then moved on to those of Marx and the Soviet Communists. The preface to his major work on education, *Trudovaya shkola,* mentions Blonskii's indebtedness for his idea of an activity school to Marx, Froebel, Pestalozzi, Scharrelmann, and Dewey.[51] Blonskii was an advocate of the Unified Labor School, together with the complex method and the science of pedology, or child study. In spite of his devotion to the Communist cause, Blonskii himself and pedology were repudiated by the Communist Party and he became a victim of the purge of 1936.[52] Thus, both Shatskii and Blonskii learned that the interests of communism are always above those of education and of the individual. Albert P. Pinkevich and Anatol V. Lunacharskii, both of whom were faithful servants of communism in their educational work, were likewise liquidated when the Soviet regime had no further use for them or their doctrines.[53] John Dewey was to learn the same thing—that with Communists it is all or nothing. He, too, was purged—not in a physical sense, fortunately—several times, during and after his lifetime.

Lunacharskii, who was appointed in 1917 as the first People's Commissar of Education (Narkompros) under the new regime, admired John Dewey and his ideas and referred to them in his writings on education.[54] Pinkevich, the rector of the Second

State University of Moscow, wrote approvingly of Dewey's educational ideas during the 1920's. In one of his pedagogical works for teachers, which was translated in 1929 by George S. Counts and Nucia P. Lodge, Pinkevich acknowledged that Dewey was one of the modern American educators who had exerted a "tremendous influence" [55] on Soviet education. According to Pinkevich, "Dewey comes infinitely closer to Marx and the Russian Communists" than any of the contemporary German educators.[56] To be identified by a leading Soviet educator as one of "the bourgeois forerunners of the true labor school" [57] was indeed profound praise for Dewey. Pinkevich, moreover, recommended that "every contemporary student of education should study his [Dewey's] writings," but warned them against his non-Marxian approach. After all, he said, "Dewey is a representative of the bourgeoisie, albeit a talented one and one who has superior grasp of contemporary industry, and therefore in his ideology a stranger to us." [58] Dedication to Communist ideology in education and in life proved to be of little avail to the major Soviet educators when the purges came. The changed political and pedagogical policies were instrumental in bringing about "the disappearance and liquidation of leading educators, among them Pinkevich, Lunacharsky, and Blonsky." [59]

Considerations of time and space make it difficult to cite and analyze other Soviet appraisals and appreciations of Dewey's educational theory and practice during the first decade or decade and a half after the Revolution. Such an analysis would be desirable in connection with obtaining a full understanding of the dynamics of the Soviet-American relationships in education during the 1920's. It is enough to call attention, at this point, to the frequent mention of Dewey in the *Pedagogical Encyclopedia* (1927) edited by Kalashnikov and Epshtein, two important figures in Soviet education.[60]

DEWEY'S VISIT TO THE U. S. S. R. Dewey finally had an opportunity to see the Soviet Union for himself early in the summer of 1928. He joined 24 other American educators on a tour under the auspices of the American Society for Cultural Relations with Russia. This trip was "entirely unofficial, the members paying their own expenses," according to Lucy Branham, secretary of the Society.[61] In announcing this tour, Miss Branham pointed out that some of the members were "authors of ideas which have been put into general practice in Russia," the foremost being Dewey, who was "as well known to Russian educators as to American." [62] In the delegation of 25 American educators were J. McKeen Cattell, editor of *School and Society;* former President Lotus D. Coffman of the University of Minnesota; President Donald J. Cowling of Carleton College; President Stephen Duggan of the Institute of International Education; Robert Gault, National Research Council and Carnegie Institution; President Parke R. Kolbe of the Brooklyn Polytechnic Institute; Joshua Kunitz, writer, lecturer, and teacher; President Kenneth G. Matheson of Drexel Institute, Philadelphia; President Emeritus George D. Olds of Amherst College; Professor Thomas Woody of the University of Pennsylvania; Miss Branham; and elementary, high school, and college instructors and administrators. The American Society for Cultural Relations with Russia gave a dinner at the Hotel Astor in New York City on December 10, 1928, to honor Dewey and his educational delegation; Dewey and others addressed this group.[63]

The group sailed on June 23, 1928, on the Drottningholm for Gothenburg, Sweden, and Dewey was to meet them in Leningrad. Although I have not been able to ascertain exactly how long the delegation remained in the Soviet Union, it is apparent that Dewey's stay was short, possibly not more than two weeks. According to his daughter, "In Russia his chief contacts were with educationists; his time there was too short for investigation of economic and political fields." [64] When the delegation arrived in Leningrad, probably early in July, the schools must have been closed for the summer.

In later years, Dewey wrote concerning his trip, but offered few concrete details regarding what he had actually accomplished or what places he had visited in the Soviet Union. "When I was in St. Petersburg [sic] and Moscow in '28 I met a number of men and women engaged in one way or another in educational activities. . . ." [65] Nor do his "Impressions of Soviet Russia," published in the *New Republic* during the months of

September and October of 1928 (reprinted in book form in the following year),[66] or other writings[67] about the Soviet Union, yield any clues. Pertinent information might be obtained from other individuals and other sources, perhaps from hitherto unpublished letters from Dewey.

The American philosopher-pedagogue made a serious effort, it would seem, to look upon the Soviet scene as objectively as possible. He speedily became aware that there was a sense of reality about Soviet life—a reality "of the present and future, the essence of the Revolution in its release of courage, energy and confidence in life." [68] He was convinced that, as far as the people of the Soviet Union were concerned, communism was "of less account than is the fact of this achieved revolution of heart and mind, this liberation of a people to consciousness of themselves as a determining power in the shaping of their ultimate fate." [69] In later passages, Dewey repeated his sincere appreciation of the changes wrought in the Russian people's lives in more or less the same terminology.[70] After the publication of his articles in the *New Republic,* however, Dewey was made aware through various comments that his statements subordinating the economic phase of the Revolution were "too sweeping." Consequently, in the book version, he found it necessary to add an explanatory footnote: "I should not think of denying that the political aspect of the economic revolution in elevating labor, especially the interests of the factory workers, from the bottom of the social scale to the top is an integral factor in the psychological and moral transformation." [71] Be that as it may, there can be little doubt of Dewey's desire to be as fair-minded as possible to the Russian Revolution and the Soviet regime.

Not that Dewey was naïve or blinded by the friendliness and attention of the people he met in Leningrad and Moscow. He was realistic enough to admit his basic limitation, namely, that "without a prolonged stay, wide contacts and a knowledge of the language, accurate information is hard to come by. One gets about as many views as there are persons one converses with, even about things that might be supposed to be matters of fact; or else one finds questions evaded in an embarrassed way." [72] As a highly sophisticated person, Dewey soon learned that the information he received was often partially true [73] and then mainly of sometime in the past, so that he felt "the necessity of giving an exact dating to every statement made about conditions in Soviet Russia." [74] I had similar experiences, but I found that Soviet educators, students, and other citizens tended to fuse the future, rather than the past, with the present.

Dewey showed that he understood the inner nature of the Soviet regime by mentioning "secret police, inquisitions, arrests and deportations of *Nepmen* and *Kulaks,* exiling of party opponents—including divergent elements in the party . . . ," but he insisted that "life for the masses goes on with regularity, safety and decorum" [75] and "even the 'wild children' . . . have now disappeared from the streets of the large cities." [76]

At Peterhof, near Leningrad, Dewey visited a colony of former "wild children," and orphaned and refugee children. Even though he knew that there was "a marked disproportion between the breadth of my conclusion and the narrowness of the experience upon which it rests," [77] he was nevertheless confident enough to say, "I have never seen anywhere in the world such a large proportion of intelligent, happy, and intelligently occupied children." [78] To Dewey, the achievements of this colony and every other "institution of children and youth which I visited" were revealing. "When their almost unimaginable earlier history and background were taken into account, the effect was to leave me with the profoundest admiration for the capacities of the people from which they sprang, and an unshakable belief in what they can accomplish." [79]

Dewey, it is obvious, spared few superlatives in setting down his impressions. He narrates that "the hours of several days of leisure time before the arrival of the party of fellow American educators in Leningrad were spent in the Hermitage." [80] The sight of groups of peasants looking at the art treasures impelled him to comment that "the like of it is not to be seen anywhere else in the world." [81] Since this experience "was repeated in every museum, artistic, scientific, historical, we visited," Dewey wondered whether "perhaps the most significant thing in Russia, after all, is not the effort at economic transformation, but the will to use an economic change as the means of developing a popular cultivation, especially an esthetic one, such as the world has never known." [82]

The impressions of the Soviet Union recorded by Dewey must be read very closely to be fully comprehended. Otherwise, one may get the feeling that at times Dewey is dazzled into dubious decisions about what he experienced, while at other times his eyes have penetrated behind the show places and the show pieces to the essence of Soviet society itself. It is possible that, as a man who was determined to be an objective onlooker, Dewey saw both the positive and the negative aspects of Soviet life and made certain to depict both. Yet, there were times when his form of expression became so forceful and forthright that there could be little doubt as to his fundamental feelings. This type of thinking is illustrated in the following paragraph.

Dewey described "a non-official visit to a House of Popular Culture," [83] presumably in Moscow. He was deeply impressed by the "fine new building," consisting of many cultural and recreational facilities and voluntarily erected and controlled by the trade unions, rather than by the government. He was certain that this House of Popular Culture had "no intrinsic and necessary connection with communistic theory and practice" [84]; and that it was in existence in Soviet cities, rather than in American industrial cities, "in a society supposedly rigidly managed by the State on the basis of dogmatic theory, as an evidence of the vitality of organized voluntary initiative and coöperative effort." [85] Apparently Dewey was not aware of the relationship of the trade unions to the Soviet government or of the connection between culture and political ideology. However, in a subsequent passage, he did analyze the significance of propaganda for Soviet education, emerging with the conclusion that in Russia "propaganda is education and education is propaganda. They are more than confounded; they are identified." [86]

There are several interesting pages in Dewey's report on Stanislav Shatskii and his educational experiments,[87] although he did not mention the distinguished Soviet educator by name until some sixty pages later. His overall judgment of Shatskii was that "his pilgrim's progress from reforming pedagogue to convinced communist affords a symbol of the social phase of the entire Soviet educational movement." [88]

Compliments to the Soviet educational system multiplied as the report proceeded. He noted "the marvelous development of progressive educational ideas and practices under the fostering care of the Bolshevist government—and I am speaking here of what I have seen and not just been told about." [89] "That which distinguishes the Soviet schools both from other national systems and from the progressive schools of other countries (with which they have much in common) is precisely the conscious control of every educational procedure by reference to a single and comprehensive social purpose." [90] The consequent weakening of the family through the school and other social agencies constitutes "a most interesting sociological experimentation." [91] The children's summer colonies which Dewey visited "compare favorably with similar institutions anywhere, with respect to food, hygiene, medical attention and daily nurture." [92] These colonies and other governmental educational projects he regarded as "a striking exemplification of the conscious and systematic utilization of the school in behalf of definite social policy. There are many elements of propaganda connected with this policy, and many of them are obnoxious to me personally. But the broad effort to employ the education of the young as a means of realizing certain social purposes cannot be dismissed as propaganda without relegating to that category all endeavor at deliberate social control." [93] With all his evident enthusiasm for the single-minded social objective in Soviet Russia, Dewey made it clear that he did not overlook the connection between Communist ideology and education. He pointed up "the central position of the schools in the production of a communist ideology as a condition of the successful operation of communist institutions." [94] To buttress this conclusion he cited a statement by Lenin "that has become a part of the canonical scriptures of Bolshevist educational literature. . . . 'The school, apart from life, apart from politics, is a lie, a hypocrisy. Bourgeois society indulged in this lie, covering up the fact that it was using the schools as a means of domination, by declaring that the school was politically neutral, and in the service of all. We must declare openly what it concealed, namely, the political function of the school. While the object of our previous struggle was to overthrow the bourgeoisie, the aim of the new generation is much more complex: It is to construct communist society.'" [95]

A careful analysis should be made of the implications of this statement, the final portion of which is strongly reminiscent of the terminology used by Premier Nikita S. Khrushchev to describe his new educational reform, as well as of that of leading Soviet educators from the time of Lenin to the present. However, Dewey chose to end one of his essays on this note, without any further comment. It seems barely conceivable that he could have approved of the vocabulary in which Lenin clothed his thoughts.

In the next essay, Dewey once more gave expression to his appreciation of Soviet education. "The Russian educational situation is enough to convert one to the idea that only in a society based upon the coöperative principle can the ideals of educational reformers be adequately carried into operation." [96] ". . . I can only pay my tribute to the liberating effect of active participation in social life upon the attitude of students. Those whom I met had a vitality and a kind of confidence in life . . . that afforded one of the most stimulating experiences of my life." [97] "All that I had ever, on theoretical grounds, believed as to the extent to which the dull and dispirited attitude of the average school is due to isolation of school from life was more than confirmed by what I saw of the opposite in Russian schools." [98] "Soviet education has not made the mistake of confusing unity of education with uniformity; on the contrary, centralization is limited to the matter of ultimate aim and spirit, while in detail diversification is permitted, or rather encouraged." [99] It is odd that Dewey did not distinguish between form and content, between the accidental and the essential. He may not have been acquainted with the statement by Stalin which his own resembled. In his address, "On the Political Task of the University of the Peoples of the East," May 18, 1925, Stalin identified "the universal human culture toward which socialism is moving" as "proletarian in content, national in form." [100] By proletarian, Stalin meant Socialist or Communist. It was evident from Stalin's address that the use of the form of national culture merely meant biding one's time until the Communists could gain full control over all minority peoples, even assimilating some of them. According to a careful and competent analyst of Soviet national policy, "Stalin's slogan of 'universal human culture' concealed the extension to non-Russian peoples of Soviet Russian culture." [101] In other words, Dewey did not appear here to grasp that what really mattered in Soviet education was the aim or spirit of communism, and all other details, diverse as they were, were to further the basic objective. Diversity and individualism per se were not acceptable to the regime.

From what Dewey wrote concerning the educational work with minority nationality groups in the Soviet Union, it is obvious that he neither observed directly, nor studied the documentary evidence, nor yet comprehended what the Russians were doing to the culture of the non-Russian population groups. To Dewey, "The idea of cultural autonomy that underlies political federation is made a reality in the schools" and "the scrupulous regard for cultural independence characteristic of the Soviet regime is one of the chief causes of its stability, in view of the non-communist beliefs of these populations." [102] Certainly, he could not predict that in a year or two the Soviet government would decree the abolition of the Arabic script of the Central Asiatic peoples of the Soviet Union and the substitution of the Roman alphabet, or the change around 1940 from the Roman to the Cyrillic alphabet, thus breaking the chain of tradition which bound the Asiatic peoples to their ancient cultural heritage. However, had he studied the question more thoroughly, he would have had to qualify the sweeping nature of his generalizations.

Laudatory statements on the educational and social system of the Soviet Union appear almost on every other page in Dewey's report. He appreciated that "the freedom from race- and color-prejudice characteristic of the regime is one of the greatest assets in Bolshevist propaganda among Asiatic peoples." [103] "In view of the prevailing idea of other countries as to the total lack of freedom and total disregard of democratic methods in Bolshevist Russia, it is disconcerting, to say the least, to anyone who has shared in that belief, to find Russian school children much more democratically organized than our own; and to note that they are receiving, through the system of school administration, a training that fits them, much more systematically than is attempted in our professedly democratic country, for later active participation in the self-direction of both local communities and industries." [104] Considering the difficulties resulting from the war, hunger, poverty, antagonistic teachers, and others, Dewey was amazed at the progress of the Soviet educational system: "It is a going concern; a self-moving organism. While an American visitor may feel a certain patriotic pride in noting in how many respects an initial impulse came from some progressive schools in our own country, he is at once humiliated and stimulated to new endeavor to see how much more organically that idea is incorporated in the Russian system than in our own." [105] Anyone with an experience similar to his own in the Soviet Union, said Dewey, "will deeply regret those artificial barriers and that barricade of false reports that now isolates American teachers from that educational system in which our professed progressive democratic ideas are most completely embodied, and from which accordingly, we might, if we would, learn much more than from the system of any other country." [106] Dewey seems to be bending sharply backward in the last three passages—praising the Soviet school system to the skies and simultaneously saying nothing good about his own. Perhaps the "American visitor" to whom he was alluding was Dewey himself expressing pleasure that his own educational ideas had been so well received in the country he had just visited. There can be no doubt at all that Dewey really meant to state his unstinted admiration for the Soviet educational system, in which "however rigid and dogmatic the Marxian symbols may be, actual practices are affected by an experimental factor that is flexible, vital, creative." [107]

In the final pages of the sixth and last essay of his "Impressions of Soviet Russia," Dewey summed up his analysis of what he had seen and heard. "There is, of course, an immense amount of indoctrination and propaganda in the schools. But if the existing tendency develops, it seems fairly safe to predict that in the end this indoctrination will be subordinate to the awakening of initiative and power of independent judgment, while coöperative mentality will be evolved. It seems impossible that an education intellectually free will not militate against a servile acceptance of dogma as dogma. One hears all the time about the dialectic movement by means of which a movement contradicts itself in the end. I think the schools are a 'dialectic' factor in the evolution of Russian communism." [108] Dewey's faith in the future of Soviet education and his optimism about the triumph of "independent judgment" over the "immense amount of indoctrination and propaganda" in the Soviet schools have not as yet been fulfilled.

Jane Dewey called her father's series of essays on his Soviet trip "very sympathetic in tone with the U. S. S. R.," a fact "which led to his being described as a 'Bolshevik' and 'red' in the conservative press." [109] It is not at all difficult to see why some would regard Dewey as a Soviet sympathizer, judging from some of the passages quoted in the previous paragraphs. It is also difficult to take issue with a contemporary commentator on Dewey who considers his Soviet reports as "jaundiced." [110] However, one should not overlook one of Dewey's concluding statements to the effect that he could not "feel sympathy" with the emphasis by Bolshevism "upon the necessity of class war and of world revolution by violence." [111]

It would be interesting to examine the Soviet periodicals, newspapers, and books, both the general and the pedagogical, to ascertain how Dewey's report was received. Very probably, there would have been some criticism of it, but it is likely that it might have been approved in general. It is worthy of note that there does not seem to be any record of its having been translated into Russian.

Apart from this report on the Soviet Union, Dewey's educational writings were being read, analyzed, and applied by the Soviet educators all through the 1920's. A more thorough research than was possible for the present essay would have doubtless disclosed numerous citations of Dewey's works in the textbooks for teachers and other pedagogical publications. But it must be mentioned once more that there do not seem to have been any translations after the second edition of G. A. Luchinskii's version of *The School and Society* in 1925.

All through the decade, Soviet educators showered considerable attention upon the Dalton Plan, or, in the picturesque words of Meyer, they "hugged the Dalton magic to their bolshevik bosoms." [112] Often, the Dalton Plan was combined with the Project and the Complex Methods. Helen Parkhurst's *Education on the Dalton Plan* (1922) and Evelyn Dewey's *The Dalton Laboratory Plan* (1922) were both translated into Russian in 1923, with Nadezhda K. Krupskaya providing "an eulogistic introduction" to the latter volume.[113] It is possible that the influence of the Dalton Plan, which stemmed from the Progressive Educational tradition of Preston W. Search of Pueblo and Frederic Burk of San Francisco, but which apparently drew upon the principles of Dewey,[114] also served as a means of transmission of Deweyan doctrines. Incidentally, there was criticism of the Dalton Plan even while it was being practiced. Thus, Pinkevich, in his textbook of pedagogy published in the mid-twenties, complained that in the Dalton Plan "there is almost no collective work of any kind" and expressed the fear that "it will be instrumental in developing individualistic tendencies in children." [115] It is also of interest that in the very popular volume, *The Diary of a Communist Schoolboy* (1928), by N. Ognyov, the leading character must have stated the criticisms of many pupils: "The Dalton thing is a wash-out. No one can understand a thing, not even the *skworkers* [schoolworkers, or teachers]. . . . The boys say that this plan was invented by some Lord Dalton of bourgeois stock. Now I wonder what the devil we need this bourgeois plan for?" [116]

The criticisms of the Dalton Plan must have been part of a much larger campaign of criticism from various Soviet sources which was directed against the various forms of Progressive Education including the Project Method of Dewey and Kilpatrick. The complaint of Pinkevich against the lack of collective work in the Dalton Plan may be regarded as foreshadowing the violent reaction to Progressive Education in the early 1930's.

The most thoroughgoing Soviet analysis of Dewey's educational thought was made by Boris B. Komarovskii (1889–   ), professor of education at the Pedagogical Institute, Baku, Azerbaizhan. As early as 1926, Komarovskii completed a doctoral dissertation at the University of Baku on the philosophic premises of Dewey's pedagogy.[117] Four years later, this educationist, who had written on educational sociology, psychology, administration, theory, and history, published an expanded version under the title, *The Educational Philosophy of John Dewey in Relation to the History of American Pedagogy*.[118] This is by far the longest, most detailed and analytic, and most objective study about Dewey by a Soviet educational specialist. Issued in an edition of 3,000 copies, this book comprises 277 pages apportioned among seven chapters and an appendix. The chapters deal with social-historical factors underlying the theory and practice of American education around the beginning of the twentieth century; the foundations of the scientific-educational theory of the U. S. A. in relation to European pedagogical theory; John Dewey's theory of education; the biological-psychological-sociological foundations of the activity school; educational sociology; the structure and maintenance of the activity school; and the philosophical foundations of the didactics of Dewey. The Appendix contains a sketch of the life, ideas, and influence of Dewey; extensive bibliographies of the literature on the history of American education, on American pedagogical theory and practice, and works by and about Dewey (including criticism) in several languages; and notes and indexes.

The chief characteristic of the book is that it quotes frequently from the original writings of Dewey, while citing Marx and Engels only twice in Chapter II and Marx and Lenin three times in Chapter VII. Komarovskii also shows much familiarity with American pedagogical literature represented by such leading educators as William H. Kilpatrick, Boyd H. Bode, David Snedden, William C. Bagley, Charles H. Judd, Isaac. L. Kandel, Herman H. Horne, Edward L. Thorndike, and others.

The tone of the book is fair-minded, and the ideas and work of Dewey are presented on a factual basis. Due to his own tradition, Komarovskii contrasts Dewey's pragmatism with Marxism and shows his preference for the latter.[119] He is thoughtful to discuss Dewey's influence on education in the United States and in foreign countries, especially England, India, and Germany.[120] Apart from attributing *Genetic Psychology,* a book he did not write, to Kilpatrick, the author seems to have made no significant error of fact. Komarovskii closes the textual part of the book with a discussion of more than five pages on Dewey's attitude toward the Russian Revolution and his relations to the Soviet Union.[121]

Komarovskii acknowledged that "Russian literature on

Dewey is exceptionally meagre." [122] He called attention to the fact that a more or less thorough study of Dewey's philosophic concepts had been made by Y. Berman in his *Sushchnost pragmatizma (Essence of Pragmatism,* 1911, pp. 86–164) and that Dewey's pedagogical thought had been interpreted by a large number of Russian educators, such as Blonskii, Krupskaya, Kalashnikov, Lunacharskii, Pinkevich, and Shulgin.

The treatment by Komarovskii of the American educator's relation to the U. S. S. R. covers Dewey's reputation, his trip to the Soviet Union in 1928, his attitude toward the Russian Revolution, and his judgment of Soviet education. The Russians' early knowledge of Dewey was derived, according to Komarovskii, from the five works of his which were translated into their language. Dewey's ideas on vocational education were generally analyzed in brief essays in terms of the Marxist philosophical framework. Citing an article published in *Pravda* (June, 1918) by Krupskaya and one by Lunacharskii in *Narodnoe Prosveshchenie* (April, 1927) as evidence, he stated that "The best experts in Soviet pedagogy regard Dewey as one of the most talented pedagogues in the world, whose educational viewpoint is closest to the Marxist theory of education." [123] One is reminded of very similar language used by Albert Pinkevich in his commendation of Dewey in his textbook for teachers.

Komarovskii went on to say that "the best representatives of Russian progressive pedagogical thought were brought up" on the first works of Dewey, which had been translated into Russian at the beginning of the twentieth century.[124] Moreover, "the strong influence of Dewey was particularly felt at the beginning of the October Revolution." [125] He mentioned specifically Pavel Blonskii, Aleksei Kalashnikov, and Stanislav Shatskii, as having been influenced at the time by Dewey's theories. Blonskii's *Reforma nauki* (1920) was close to the point of view of Dewey's *Reconstruction in Philosophy,* according to Komarovskii, who proceeded to point up some similarities between Dewey and Shatskii and Kalashnikov. After the initial years of the Revolution, in 1922, Komarovskii maintains that there was a reduction of interest in Dewey, since the Soviet pedagogues were seriously concerned at the time about defining the differences between the capitalistic and Communistic systems of education. Komarovskii's own doctoral dissertation in 1926 on Dewey was, of course, evidence of Soviet interest, but, after Dewey's visit to Soviet Russia two years later, the pedagogues of the U. S. S. R. participated in a revival of interest in Dewey's thought, particularly when they were seeking a theoretical basis for their new methods of teaching. Komarovskii also cited an unnamed educator who reflected the Soviet attitude toward Dewey in 1928: "Dewey is a timid, indecisive conciliator. He is a man of profound reason, but weak in the political sense of the term. Rather than criticize the capitalistic system of society, Dewey offers a cloudy conception of democracy, which does not commit anyone (even Dewey himself) to anything. His democracy is a form of easy refuge, like Christianity. In form, Dewey's conception is in contradiction to imperialism and exploitation, while in reality his international democracy upholds the ruling imperialism." [126] This writer then wondered whether Dewey, following the example of Hegel (as stated by Heine), did not consciously obscure his theories.

The signs of the future were evident, as far as the Soviet attitude to Dewey was concerned. That Dewey was appreciated and valued could be seen. Yet, there were serious reservations about him, particularly his lack of a Marxist philosophical orientation. And the references to "imperialism," while not seasoned with venom, were promises of what was yet to come.

DE-DEWEYIZATION, 1931–37. The movement against Progressive Education was gathering momentum and, around 1930, was coming to a head. Even while the clouds were darkening, the *Great Soviet Encyclopedia* could describe John Dewey in 1931 as "an outstanding American philosopher, psychologist, sociologist, and pedagog." [127] In an article of close to three columns, the encyclopedia summed up Dewey's philosophical position in a reasonable and serious manner, taking care to point out that "in Dewey's treatment of social problems, the petty bourgeois frame of mind can be clearly seen" and that "Dewey does not conceal his dislike of the theory of revolutionary Marxism." [128] Anyone familiar with Dewey's thought can recognize the description of it in this article, but again a warning is given with reference to the bourgeois nature of that thought:

"Despite his clear understanding of the contradictions of capitalism, Dewey looks upon education as a true bourgeois-liberal: education must contribute to the toning down of class contradictions, and it must help the capitalists preserve their ruling position." [129] Appreciation of the significance of Dewey's educational theory alternates with Marxian criticism. "The uniqueness of Dewey's educational viewpoint lies in the conjunction of an interpretation of education as an active, practical affair and the high valuation of its intellectual factors. . . . While overflowing with valuable observations, ideas and generalizations, Dewey's educational theory, however, not only does not aim at awakening in students a consciously critical attitude toward the social foundations of bourgeois society, but, on the contrary, sees the activity system of education as the best means of toning down, i.e., of concealing class antagonisms." [130] As Professor Levit analyzes this brief essay on Dewey, "Despite the fact that the article contains some errors, half-truths and ambiguities, one gets the feeling that the object described (Dewey's philosophy) could be recognized when encountered, especially if one kept in mind the fact that the description had been made by a Soviet Marxist." [131]

The official break with Progressive Education can be traced to a resolution "On the Primary and Secondary School," [132] passed on September 1, 1931, by the Central Committee of the Communist Party of the Soviet Union. This decree laid down the principle that the schools must do more serious work than previously, since the Project Method and other Progressive procedures had failed to give students the fundaments and to prepare them properly for the tekhnikums and for higher education. The Soviet frame of mind was well illustrated by the remark of Pinkevich: " . . . unfortunate results showed that the project method and the Dalton Plan do not provide sound and profound knowledge, and do not train the children to work systematically." [133]

Progressive Education could not supply the demand for the trained personnel required for the fulfillment of the Five Year Plan. Many young people who left school, "although on the whole well adjusted to their environment and keenly interested in actual problems, proved to lack the most elementary knowledge." [134] The Communist Party finally decided to bring back Leninism to education and to get rid of foreign pedagogical methods. From this point onward, the influence of foreign educational theory and practice began to wane. Along with the decline of foreign educational influence in the Soviet Union went the lowering of status of such Soviet educators as Shatskii and Blonskii who had drawn inspiration from foreign pedagogues.

A follow-up resolution, "On School Programs and Administration in Primary and Secondary Schools," [135] passed on August 25, 1932, by the Central Committee, criticized the teaching of a number of subjects and ordered forthwith a revision of the entire primary and secondary school curricula. It became clear that the authority of teachers and principals replaced the principle of pupil freedom and that proper conduct, discipline, and standards would now be paramount in Soviet schools. The Commissar of the People's Education (Narkompros), Andrei S. Bubnov, a political favorite of Stalin, expressed explicitly the Communist Party's new line in education later in 1932 in an address to regional commissars and other educational officials as follows: "Our next task is to re-establish discipline in the schools," inasmuch as "without planned discipline properly imparted to the students there will never be a real Soviet education." [136]

The new educational reforms began in the fall of 1932. The "brigade system" and the Project Method were scrapped, the teacher resumed his traditional role of disciplinarian, the Three R's were once more emphasized, non-essential subjects were relegated to the background, and written examinations were once again given at the end of the school year. [137] The decree of the Central Committee of the Communist Party, February 12, 1933, "On Textbooks for the Elementary School," demanded that "real textbooks" be written at once to take the place of the many pamphlets and manuals which "do not impart systematic knowledge of the curricula." [138] It was such "brand new school books, prepared by Soviet scholars in a six-month period of feverish labor, which the pupils found waiting for them when they began their classes" on September 1, 1933. [139] Furthermore, the subjects of history and geography, "which had been lost in the maze of 'conferences' and 'projects,'" were differentiated, and new separate texts were made available.[140]

What might be called the era of de-Deweyization of the Soviet educational system was decidedly related to the internal and external crisis experienced by the Soviet government during the 1930's. One has merely to remember the frequent and violent political purges that accompanied the general political transition from the influence of Lenin and Trotsky to that of Stalin. This period, which lasted from about 1931 to 1937, was also marked by the recognition of the Soviet Union by the United States in 1933; the promulgation of the New Stalin Constitution of 1936; and the publication in 1938 of the *History of the Communist Party of the Soviet Union (Bolsheviks): Short Course,* a volume authorized for purposes of indoctrination by the Central Committee, prepared by a committee of historians under Andrei A. Zhdanov, and supervised, edited and allegedly even written by Joseph V. Stalin. This historical work, which became the bible of Soviet propaganda, was designed "to establish the role of Stalin in the October Revolution and to provide historical justification for Stalin's personal dictatorship." [141]

Under these circumstances, and in spite of the good will that supposedly went along with American recognition of the Soviet regime, Progressive Education and the Deweyan doctrines had no chance for survival. The political guillotine began to hack away with greater frequency and severity at foreign educational doctrines and at the heads, figuratively and even literally, of the Soviet educators who had espoused them. On May 16, 1934, V. Molotov, chairman of the Council of the People's Commissars of the U. S. S. R., and J. Stalin, in his capacity as secretary of the Central Committee of the Communist Party of the Soviet Union, signed two decrees which laid down the Party line "On the Teaching of Civic History in the Schools of the U. S. S. R." and "On the Teaching of Geography in the Elementary and Secondary Schools of the U. S. S. R." [142] On September 3, 1935, a joint decree by the Council of People's Commissars of the U. S. S. R. and the Central Committee of the Communist party gave definite instructions "On the Organization of Educational Work and Inner Order in the Primary, Incomplete Secondary, and Secondary School." [143] This regulation brought back the five-point grading system of tsarist Russia and indicated the precise steps to be taken in evaluating students for promotion and for entrance into higher educational institutions.

The Communist party now made its full power felt all through the Soviet educational system. These laws and others preceding and following them constituted excellent evidence of the emphasis "on the ever-increasing role of the teacher as a fighter for communist education of the new generation." [144]

Finally, on July 4, 1936, "the death blow for progressive education" [145] came with the resolution by the Central Committee of the Communist Party "On the Pedagogical Perversions in the System of the Narkompros." [146] This decree labeled Blonskii's favorite discipline of pedology as pseudo-scientific and anti-Marxist, forbade its further application, and condemned its proponents. Furthermore, the new law put an end to the intelligence tests and the other types of psychological measurement, with the result that psychology, the role of which was recognized all over the world as having relevance to education, was no longer to play a role in the Soviet school. [147] Prominent Soviet educators such as Blonskii, Lunacharskii, and Pinkevich fell victims to the new political-educational policy which reflected a revival of the spirit of nationalism in the Soviet Union. Pinkevich, who had visited the University of Cincinnati in the spring of 1929 in order to study President Herman Schneider's well-known work-study program, [148] in time began to de-Deweyize himself by omitting, except for one reference, any mention of Dewey in *Science and Education in the U. S. S. R.* (English translation, 1935). Unfortunately for him, this proved to be of no avail in saving his status.

To replace the pedagogical pioneers, the Communists brought to the fore Anton Semyonovich Makarenko, who became known as "the outstanding Soviet pedagogue." [149] Makarenko, who won fame for his practical work with juvenile criminals, as well as for such writings as *The Road to Life* and *A Book for Parents,* turned out to be "the only figure from the early period of revolutionary idealism and educational experimentation who weathered the political storms and the radical changes in educational policy of the 1930's." [150] Although "the reputations of Blonskii, Shul'gin, and many others [had] wilted under the blaze of more recently proclaimed truths," [151] the name of Makarenko began to rise from relative obscurity at the time when educational theory and practice underwent a transformation, since the new order in Soviet education "coincided with the trend of his own thought." [152] It is noteworthy that Makarenko, whose significance seems to have escaped foreign writers on Soviet education before 1940, has been catapulted into the status of being recognized internationally as *the* Soviet educator.

Ironically enough, Stalin's educational hatchet man, Andrei S. Bubnov, the People's Commissar of Education, was dismissed from his position in October, 1937. Even such a fully faithful follower of the leader as Bubnov could not survive in a totalitarian society. Since his successor, Vladimir P. Potemkin, was a historian and a teacher, and the founder of the Academy of the Pedagogical Sciences in 1943, it is likely that the Communist party felt that education must be under the supervision of a man who was not merely a loyal Party member but also a properly qualified educator. [153]

The new Soviet educational policy caused surprise and chagrin among American Progressive educators. During the heyday of experimentation in Soviet education, Progressive pedagogues in the United States looked upon the Soviet school system as "an educational Mecca" and "annually, boatloads of American teachers flocked to Russia to observe Progressive Education at work." [154] Even though some publicized their disapproval of the Soviet political line, "in the end all seemed to agree that by virtue of Progressive Education the Russian schools were leaping into world leadership." [155] But the decrees of the Central Committee of the Communist party from 1931 onwards caught the American Progressives with their pedagogical plans down. In the colorful words of Meyer, "Naturally, the action of the committee was a bitter pill for the rank and file of the American progressives to swallow. For years they had been cackling about the wide acceptance and steady advance of their theories in Russia. For years, too, they had been pointing to the Soviets as the shining example of what could be done when a whole nation installed Progressive Education in its public schools. And then, suddenly, the Soviets deserted and went over to the enemy. It was, to say the least, most unkind." [156]

It is one of the ironies of history that after pedology had been liquidated in the middle 1930's, "there began a period of more or less normal 'Western' pre-school policy, with stress upon play, music, etc. Toys, dolls, fairy-tales—all of which had previously been banished—reappeared together with childish fun and laughter," [157] reported a Soviet teacher. The educational authorities organized at once conferences and special courses to enable kindergarten teachers and workers with young children to reorient and thereby to requalify themselves in accordance with the pedagogical principles of the new Party line. [158]

THE TROTSKY INVESTIGATION. Although the reputation of Dewey as an educator was considerably dimmed by the changes in Communist party policy with respect to the Soviet school system, the man himself was apparently held in respect. However, the events from about 1936 onward brought about a rapid change in the Soviet attitude toward John Dewey.

In 1936, the Moscow Trials, as they were known all over the world, which involved charges against such leading Communists as Lev B. Kamenev and Grigori Zinoviev, commanded considerable interest. Leon D. Trotsky, against whom Stalin proceeded in 1925, a little over a year after the death of Lenin, was accused of hatching a conspiracy to assassinate Stalin. Events moved with great rapidity: [159] Trotsky was dismissed from the Politbureau (1926), from the Central Committee (October, 1927), and finally from the Party itself (November, 1927). In December, 1927, Trotsky was exiled to Alma-Ata, the capital of Kazakhstan in Soviet Central Asia, and in January, 1929, Stalin ordered the deportation of Trotsky. From Turkey, the deposed Communist leader went to Norway and finally to Mexico, his apparent haven. But the long arm of the Communist regime of Soviet Russia continued to strike at Trotsky in a variety of ways.* Even while he was in Mexico, charges were made in Moscow that he had arranged for assassins to try to murder Stalin and that he had made attempts to get foreign powers to attack the Soviet Union.

Since it was evident that Trotsky would have no opportunity

* In due time, after all of Trotsky's children had died under suspicious circumstances, the sentence of death by Moscow was apparently carried out in Mexico in August, 1940, by a man who was alleged to be an agent of the Communists.

to defend himself at an open trial, some American liberals and sympathizers established the American Committee for the Defense of Leon Trotsky. John Dewey, who was a member of this committee, became its honorary chairman. When this committee set up a Commission of Inquiry in March, 1937, to examine the charges against Trotsky, Dewey consented to be the chairman of the commission and to hold hearings in Mexico, since Trotsky was unable to get even a temporary visa to another country.[160] Dewey, who was already 78 years of age, made his decision in spite of the fact that he was working on a major book, *Logic: The Theory of Inquiry*,[161] and "the intensity and variety of the pressures he had to withstand, not least from the members of his immediate family, some of whom feared he might be killed in the excitable political milieu of Mexico City." [162]

As soon as it was known that John Dewey was to travel as the chairman of the Commission of Inquiry's sub-commission to conduct hearings on the Trotsky case in Mexico, the Communists did their best to discourage him by offering him a first-class tour of the Soviet Union in order to revisit the school system. When this tactic failed, the Communist press began to circulate reports that Dewey was senile and that he was accordingly not intellectually responsible any more.[163] That this was pure fabrication was evident from the fact that Dewey's *Logic: The Theory of Inquiry* (1938) was published during the time he was alleged to have attained the status of senility. In the midst of all the pressure, "Dewey made up his mind irrevocably only after he became aware of the efforts and far-flung stratagems of the Communist party to *prevent* him from going." [164]

At the beginning of April, 1937, then, Dewey, Benjamin Stolberg, Suzanne LaFollette, George Noack, Pearl Kluger, and James T. Farrell, the well-known novelist, undertook the long and arduous train trip to Mexico. On the train, according to an eyewitness, James T. Farrell, Dewey did a great amount of work, such as reading the official versions of the first two Moscow Trials and some of the writings of Trotsky.

The sub-commission, in the words of the official report which was written by Dewey, "did not regard Mr. Trotsky as defendant or accused;" it ". . . was in Mexico neither as prosecutor or judge" but rather "solely as an investigating body, to take Mr.

Trotsky's testimony on the accusations made against him in the confessions of the Moscow defendants; to accept such documents as he had to submit in his own defense; and to report to the full commission on the basis of this evidence our decision whether or not Mr. Trotsky has a case warranting further investigation."[165] Thirteen hearings—twelve each of three hours' length and a final hearing of five hours' duration—were held during April 10–17, 1937, at the home of Diego Rivera, where Trotsky lived, in Coyacán in the presence of representatives of the Mexican and the foreign press. The sub-commission consisted of Dewey, chairman; Suzanne LaFollette, secretary; Otto Ruehle, an exiled German socialist; Benjamin Stolberg, the journalist; and Carleton Beals, specialist on Latin America, who resigned on April 17 after a disagreement with his colleagues regarding his technique of putting questions to Trotsky.

In his opening remarks on the first day, Dewey stated the sub-commission's conviction that "no man should be condemned without a chance to defend himself." [166] At the conclusion of his preliminary talk, he said "I have given my life to the work of education, which I have conceived to be that of public enlightenment in the interest of society. If I finally accepted the responsible post I now occupy, it was because I realized that to act otherwise would be to be false to my life-work." [167]

At the final session of the hearings, April 17, Trotsky summed up the case in his own behalf and concluded by expressing "my profound respect to the educator, philosopher, and personification of great American idealism, the scholar who heads the work of your Commission." [168] Trotsky's "respect for and gratitude to Dewey were personal," since "he was impressed neither by the style nor the thought" in the works of Dewey which he had read.[169] For his part, Dewey said that "he had always disagreed with Trotsky, and that after the Coyacán Hearings, he disagreed more than ever." [170] The basic disagreement between Dewey and Trotsky on the relation of means and ends in moral values and action, with specific reference to the class struggle, was clearly evident in Dewey's critical analysis in the *New International* (August, 1938) of Trotsky's earlier article in the same journal (February, 1938). Over a decade later,

Dewey remarked to James T. Farrell that Trotsky was "tragic," a person of "such brilliant native intelligence locked up in absolutes." [171]

On May 9, 1937, at a mass meeting at the Mecca Temple in New York City, Dewey publicly delivered the preliminary report and address on the Mexico hearings to the American Committee for the Defense of Leon Trotsky. After describing the scope and methods of the hearings and the nature of the oral and documentary testimony, as well as the circumstances of the resignation of Carleton Beals, Dewey concluded in behalf of the four-person sub-commission that the record indicated that "Mr. Trotsky has established a case amply warranting further investigation," and recommended that "the work of this commission proceed to its conclusion." [172]

Following the reading of this report, Dewey went on to elaborate his reasoning, and presumably that of his colleagues, in continuing the investigation. "The public record of Trotsky extending over a long period of years stands in striking contrast to the charges upon which he was convicted of plotting terrorism, assassination, industrial sabotage, wholesale wrecking, and selling out the U. S. S. R. to Hitler, Nazi Germany, and Imperial Japan. The official reports of the Moscow trials show the absence of cross-examination upon every vital point as well as many gaps, inconsistencies and contradictions." [173] Furthermore, "To hold Trotsky guilty of the specific charges upon which he was convicted because of his well-known opposition to the present rulers of the U. S. S. R. is not fair or square. It is even less so because his public record is that of unswerving, constant appeal for support of the Socialist revolution and the Socialist U. S. S. R." [174]

Dewey lashed out against those Communists, native and foreign, and liberals who were opposed to or were "luke-warm" about the investigation. Such liberals "take the stand that in any case the U. S. S. R. is the one workers' republic in the whole world; the one successful attempt of all history to build a Socialist society. Even though not themselves Communist, they want the experiment which is going on in Russia to have a fair chance. They do not want its course made harder than it is. I can understand this attitude. It has been and is my own." [175]

However, he insisted that the honest liberals who were opposed to his inquiry suffered "from the intellectual and moral confusion that is the great weakness of the professed liberals," inasmuch as "Trotsky was not convicted upon charges of theoretical and practical opposition to the regime which exists in the Soviet Union," but rather on the basis of "certain definite charges whose truth or falsity is a matter of objective fact." [176]

Either Leon Trotsky is guilty of plotting wholesale assassination, systematic wreckage with destruction of life and property; of treason of the basest sort in conspiring with political and economic enemies of the U. S. S. R. in order to destroy Socialism; or he is innocent. If he is guilty, no condemnation can be too severe. If he is innocent, there is no way in which the existing regime in Soviet Russia can be acquitted of deliberate, systematic persecution and falsification. These are important alternatives for those to face who are sympathetic with the efforts to build a Socialist State in Russia. The easier and lazier course is to avoid facing the alternatives. But unwillingness to face the unpleasant is a standing weakness with liberals. They are only too likely to be brave when affairs are going smoothly and then to shirk when unpleasant conditions demand decision and action. I cannot believe that a single genuine liberal would, if he once faced the alternatives, hold that persecution and falsification are a sound basis upon which to build an enduring Socialist society. [177]

In closing, Dewey said that "while we are not all from Missouri, most American citizens are close enough to its border to want to be shown when elementary human decency, justice and historic truth are at stake," that "friendship for truth comes before friendship for individuals and factions," and that he and his colleagues were "committed to one end and one end only: discovery of the truth as far as that is humanly possible." [178] He made a definite distinction "between fair play and a love of darkness that is reactionary in effect no matter what banner it flaunts." [179] His final sentence was a quotation from Zola in the Dreyfus case, "Truth is on the march and nothing will stop it." [180]

The investigation continued in New York City, Mexico, and Paris. Otto Ruehle, who lived in Mexico City, was authorized by the sub-commission to continue the inquiry and to furnish to his colleagues certified copies or translations of pertinent documents in the archives in Mexico which Trotsky placed at the commission's disposal. European sub-commissions were authorized to examine Trotsky's archives in Europe, which the Soviet exile gave the inquirers permission to consult.[181] The whole investigation lasted about nine months, as Dewey told Agnes E. Meyer at its conclusion. The commission "collected many scores of affidavits and depositions and examined hundreds of letters and documents, as well as making a complete analysis of the testimony given in the Moscow trials." [182]

On December 12, 1937, in an address in New York City, Dewey announced the decision of the Commission of Inquiry that Trotsky and his son Sedov were not guilty. "The implications of this finding are profoundly disturbing," since the Soviet regime "is seeking to identify political opposition to itself with criminal activity against the Soviet Union and people. . . . Shocking is the systematic use by the Communist parties throughout the world of the vicious 'Trotskyist-terrorist-fascist' amalgam as a means of destroying political opposition and even of justifying gross frameups and assassinations. . . . Even in this country, the Communist Party and its labor and liberal sympathizers have used this strictly amoral tactic, indistinguishable from the tactic of Fascism, to slander and persecute opposition, with a resulting confusion and disruption of the forces of economic and political progress which cannot be too strongly condemned." [183] The Communists, Dewey stressed, have through such conduct shown that they repudiated the principles of truth and justice which are basic to civilization. This mode of behavior which indicated to him a betrayal of the idealistic foundations of the Russian Revolution, constituted "a danger against which our own people must guard themselves without illusion and without compromise." [184]

To Agnes E. Meyer, Dewey emphasized that the commission's decision came "as a result of its prolonged, thorough, and impartial investigation—for none of its members is a Trotskyite or affiliated in any way with his theories and activities." [185] He went on to say that "the great lesson" of "these amazing revelations" in the Trotsky inquiry was "that complete breakdown of revolutionary Marxism," and that "the great lesson for all American radicals and for all sympathizers with the U. S. S. R. is that they must go back and reconsider the whole question of means of bringing about social changes and of truly democratic methods of approach to social progress."[186] Noting that "The dictatorship of the proletariat has led and, I am convinced, always must lead to a dictatorship over the proletariat and over the party," he said flatly that "democracy in the Soviet Union is a farce."[187] In point of actual fact, "While the U. S. S. R. proclaims complete freedom of the individual as its end, the means they use violate every elementary freedom of thought, speech, press, and freedom of movement, since they have revived the system that obtained under the Tsars of demanding passports for domestic travel."[188] These were harsh and shocking words on the part of a man of world-wide reputation who had hitherto "not taken a hostile position to the Soviet Union and was one of the earliest public figures to call for its recognition."[189]

Dewey saw very clearly the similarity between the methods of repression practiced in Russia and those in force in Nazi Germany. He was prophet enough to foresee by close to two years that "if war is delayed for a few years, it is not inconceivable that Russia and Germany will again be allies. We have to face this possibility."[190] Consequently, he warned that "we must stop looking to the Soviet Union as a model for solving our own economic difficulties and as a source of defense for democracy against fascism."[191] Few students of history will deny that Dewey scored here a bull's-eye. One might raise the question why it took Dewey so long to see the light. Perhaps he was keeping his mind as open as possible in line with his own convictions regarding the sifting and weighing of all pertinent evidence. This is certainly a praiseworthy ideal, but it is hard to believe that Dewey could not have arrived at a similar conclusion about the Soviet Union on the basis of the evidence available even before the Trotsky inquiry. Is it really necessary to have a complete investigation, such as conducted by Dewey, to determine when a nation is guilty of serious crimes against humanity, if sufficient, relevant, and objectively authenticated evidence is at hand? Must a thinker suspend his judgment until *all* evidence is made available? At any rate, the results of the Dewey inquiry were enlightening to fence-sitters and helped fix the future attitude of the Soviet and the other Communists toward him and his work.

It is instructive to let Dewey speak for himself with regard to his disappointment at the way Soviet Russia developed after the Revolution and especially since his visit to that country in 1928.

These revelations have been a bitter disillusionment to me personally. I always felt that the traditions of Russia and our own country were so unlike each other that we could not borrow from them in a literal way. But I did believe that a highly important social experiment was going on in that country from which we and the other so-called capitalistic nations could learn a great deal. I looked upon the Soviet Union as a social laboratory in which significant experiments would be worked out. Before the depression, that is, long before the day of conversion arrived for so many of our young literary people, in 1928 to be exact, I visited the Soviet Union and upon my return wrote a series of articles in which I presented the favorable aspects of what was being accomplished there in the educational and cultural fields in such a way that I was denounced as a Red and a Bolshevist.

I devoted my time to the study of the schools, what was being done for the spread of culture through the masses, making no study of the economic conditions. In spite of the undue prevalence of propaganda in the schools, I was genuinely impressed by the hopeful and, at the time, relatively free attitude of the young people. Although I made no examination of political conditions, I was not then aware how impossible it is for any traveler or tourist to get into any touch whatsoever with political methods.

That was before the initiation of the first five-year plan. Everything tightened up under the pressure of the five-year plans. But I have no doubt now that the causes of the increased political restrictions which have finally established a reign of terror were already at work. Naturally they have affected the whole educational system. Propaganda and regimentation have grown enormously. So much so, that the pupils are now even put into uniforms. The germs of educational freedom which certainly existed in the better schools at that time have been, according to reliable report, all but completely destroyed.

I have learned to have a great respect for the capabilities of the Russian people. In spite of the present black outlook I still am unable to surrender the faith. But how a change can be brought about under the present conditions of suppression of individuality, falsifications, and terrorism I have not the faintest conception. A people that is kept in systematic ignorance of what is going on in the world and even in their own country and which is fed on lies has lost the fundamental leverage of progress. To me, as an educator, this is the great tragedy of the Russian situation.

I find it equally disheartening when in our country, some professed liberals have come to believe that for reasons of expediency our own people should be kept in the dark as to the actual situation in Russia. For truth, instead of being a bourgeois virtue, is the mainspring of all human progress.[192]

Two reports were published by the Commission of Inquiry. The first, *The Case of Leon Trotsky,* a report of the hearings, appeared in 1937, while the final report, *Not Guilty,* was issued in 1938. The latter, according to James T. Farrell, was " a model for any future efforts of its kind, . . . an achievement in itself, . . . a monument to all who worked in this enterprise, . . . an example of democratic thinking, reasoning, procedure and of Dewey's own conceptions of free inquiry." [193] While most of the work was done by Suzanne LaFollette, Dewey contributed some of the writing and did editorial work on the report.

In evaluating the events of the Trotsky case, Farrell, who was close to Dewey during the entire inquiry, concluded that Dewey "had given himself to what he saw as truth, justice, fair play. He had put aside his own work in order to help a man whose ideas he opposed, gain a fair hearing before world history. He had given his mind fully to this cause. He practiced his own preaching in the face of scorn. At a time when so many American liberals were surrendering their best traditions to a new barbarism, he helped to vindicate those traditions." [194] In a word, Dewey, "the heir of Zola . . . had stood up and declared to the world that a mighty and powerful empire had lied, and that it had framed innocent men." [195] Finally, "the tradition which John Dewey vindicated and personified in Mexico was one which makes it possible for men to live a life of freedom based on truth. The methods which he vindicated were his own methods of free inquiry. . . . The Moscow Trials produced one of the most monstrous of all totalitarian lies. And it was with Dewey's own method of free inquiry that this lie was exposed. In substance, John Dewey revealed here, as he has in his entire life, the great moral value of the liberal ideals of truth, freedom, fair play." [196]

Even when allowance is made for the hero-worship of Dewey

which is evident in Farrell's writing, there remains a feeling of admiration for the obstinate drive of an elderly, armchair professor in behalf of the principle of justice. This was an act of will, of inner necessity. It certainly was not incumbent upon *John Dewey*, as distinct from other philosophers and liberals, to take and hold on to the initiative in the matter of weighing the guilt or the innocence of a man who was sworn to uproot the ideals of law, justice, freedom, and democracy which were rooted in Dewey's tradition and existence.

As may be surmised, the reaction of the Communists and other blind sympathizers with the Soviet Union to the Dewey activities and his report was a negative one. It varied from mild disapproval to thoroughgoing denunciation. In *Science and Society: A Marxian Quarterly*, V. J. McGill, assistant professor of philosophy at Hunter College, an editor of that periodical, contented himself with a gross understatement, saying that, despite the greater progress by the Soviet Union since 1928 in industry, science, culture, etc., than any other country, "Professor Dewey is now far less sympathetic than ten years ago." [197] The challenge by Dewey of the allegations against Trotsky in the Moscow Trials resulted in a "furor aroused among intellectuals" [198] on the college campuses. It was bad enough, from the standpoint of the sympathizers with the Soviet Union, that Dewey undertook the Trotsky inquiry, but the exposé of Stalin's justice and the complete exoneration of Trotsky were "more than Stalin's American friends could stand. The denunciation of Dewey was immediate and continuous, first coming from Corliss Lamont, a lecturer in philosophy at Columbia University, who was chairman of the Friends of the Soviet Union," [199] which became known after the German attack on Soviet Russia in 1941 as the National Council of American-Soviet Friendship.

Although Dewey used questionable judgment in waiting an inordinate length of time before publicly revealing the totalitarian nature of the U. S. S. R., he did see the relationship between Fascism and Communism. As far back as the fall of 1932, when he began to serve as chairman of a committee of the New York Teachers Union which heard charges against Left Wing members, Dewey "made his stand absolutely clear" [200] on the nature of Communism. Two years later, he issued "his classic statement on the link between fascism and communism"[201] in the *Modern Monthly:* "I am firmly convinced that imminent civil war, or even the overt threat of such a war, in a western nation, will bring Fascism with its terrible engines of oppression to power. Communism, then, with its doctrine of the necessity of the forcible overthrow of the state by armed insurrection, with its doctrine of the dictatorship of the proletariat, with its threat to exclude all other classes from civil rights, to smash their parties, and to deprive them of freedom of speech, press, assembly—which the Communists now claim for themselves under capitalism—Communism is itself, an unwitting, but none-theless powerful factor in bringing about Fascism. As an unalterable opponent of Fascism in every form, I cannot be a Communist."[202] With such an accurate insight into the character of communism, it is difficult to explain the fact that Dewey's disillusionment with the Soviet Union came more than three and a half years later.

DEWEY AND MARXISM. The relation of Dewey to Marxism as a philosophy has been explored, in greater or in lesser depth, by several writers. In his famous intellectual autobiography, published in 1930, the American philosopher nowhere mentioned Karl Marx or any Marxist thinker. He wrote of the appeal of the ideas of Hegel for him: "Hegel's synthesis of the subject and object, matter and spirit, the divine and the human, was . . . no mere intellectual formula; it operated as an immense release, a liberation. Hegel's treatment of human culture, of institutions and the arts, involved the same dissolution of hard-and-fast dividing walls, and had a special attraction for me."[203] Although Dewey "drifted away from Hegelianism,"[204] he did not deny "that acquaintance with Hegel has left a permanent deposit in my thinking."[205] While he rejected the form, or "schematism" of Hegel, he admitted that "in the content of his ideas there is often an extraordinary depth; in many of his analyses, taken out of their mechanical dialectical setting, an extraordinary acuteness. Were it possible for me to be a devotee of any system, I still should believe that there is a greater richness and greater variety of insight in Hegel than any other single systematic philosopher. . . ."[206] There is a possibility that this estimate of Hegel might have made for an understanding of, if not actually a sympathy with, the Marxian form of Hegelianism.

There do not appear to be many references in Dewey's philosophical writings to Marx, Marxism, or Soviet Russia. Dewey's dedication to democracy often acted as a brake upon any possible admiration for the theory and practice of Marxism. In 1930, he wrote that he could not "obtain intellectual, moral or esthetic satisfaction from the professed philosophy which animates Bolshevist Russia," [207] but he could still be amazed at the extent to which "organized planning" could propel the Russians ahead of the nations who had hitherto been more advanced in technical fields. To take advantage both of the principles of democracy and the (to him) demonstrated results of the Soviet government, he offered a kind of Hegelian synthesis: "A coordinating and directive council in which captains of industry and finance would meet with representatives of labor and public officials to plan the regulation of industrial activity would signify that we had entered constructively and voluntarily upon the road which Soviet Russia is traveling with so much attendant destruction and violence." [208] One might note here that Dewey by no means favored the class struggle as conceived by the Marxists.[209] According to Sidney Hook, Dewey never ignored the existence of the class struggle phenomenon in society. However, Dewey stressed "class struggles in their *plural* form . . . not only between capitalist and worker but workers, farmers, unemployed, etc." [210] Since this usage of the term "class struggle" would no doubt be unacceptable to a Marxist, it would be safe to say that Dewey had no use for the Communist idea of bringing about a fundamental change in the social order through the principle of the fundamental conflict between one level of society and the other.

Professor Sidney Hook refers to Dewey's *Liberalism and Social Action* (1935) as "a book which may well be to the twentieth century what Marx and Engels' *Communist Manifesto* was to the nineteenth. . . ." [211] Dewey, in an undated letter to Jim Cork, an American Socialist, expressed the belief that "on the basis of *Liberalism and Social Action,* and to some extent *Individualism Old and New,* I can be classed as a democratic socialist." [212] He also stated that "probably my experimentalism goes deeper than any other . . ." theory.[213]

In one passage in *Liberalism and Social Action,* Dewey expresses his opposition to any form of dictatorship, whether of the Right or of the Left.

To profess democracy as an ultimate ideal and the suppression of democracy as a means to the ideal may be possible in a country that has never known even rudimentary democracy, but when professed in a country that has anything of a genuine democratic spirit in its traditions, it signifies desire for possession and retention of power by a class, whether that class be called Fascist or Proletarian. In the light of what happens in non-democratic countries, it is pertinent to ask whether the rule of a class signifies the dictatorship of the majority, or dictatorship over the chosen class by a minority party; whether dissenters are allowed even within the class the party claims to represent; and whether the development of literature and the other arts proceeds according to a formula prescribed by a party in conformity with a doctrinaire dogma of history and of infallible leadership, or whether artists are free from regimentation? Until these questions are satisfactorily answered, it is permissible to look with considerable suspicion upon those who assert that suppression of democracy is the road to the adequate establishment of genuine democracy. The one exception—and that apparent rather than real—to dependence upon organized intelligence as the method for directing social change is found when society through an authorized majority has entered upon the path of social experimentation leading to great social change, and a minority refuses by force to permit the method of intelligent action to go into effect. Then force may be intelligently employed to subdue and disarm the recalcitrant minority.[214]

This statement must have been written about the time Dewey published his classic definition of the lack of fundamental distinction between fascism and communism in the *Modern Monthly.* There are similarities in thought and vocabulary, even though Dewey did not identify communism specifically by name in the book, as he had in the article. Moreover, there is no direct reference to the practice of communism in Soviet Russia.

In *Freedom and Culture* (1939), Dewey presented a critique of some length of the theory of Marxism and its application in the form of communism in the Soviet Union.[215] Dewey objected to the absolutistic nature of Marxism: "The inherent theoretical weakness of Marxism is that it supposed a generalization that was made at a particular date and place (and made even then only by bringing observed facts under a premise drawn from a metaphysical source) can obviate the need for continued resort to observation, and to continual revision of generalizations in their office of working hypotheses. In the name of science, a thoroughly anti-scientific procedure was formulated, in accord with which a generalization is made having the nature of ultimate 'truth,' and hence holding good at all times and places." [216] This statement strikes with force at the root of one of the sacred cows of the Soviet intellectual, namely, that Marxism-Leninism is a scientifically formulated position. Dewey saw through the Communist pretensions and called a fiction a fiction. "It is ironical that the theory which has made the most display and the greatest pretense of having a scientific foundation should be the one which has violated most systematically every principle of scientific method." [217]

Dewey pointed out the connection between the theory of Marxism and its manifestation in practice. "A monistic theory is accompanied in its practical execution by one-party control of press, schools, radio, the theater and every means of communication, even to effective restrictions imposed on private gatherings and private conversations." [218] This is a terse, but telling description of a totalitarian society which is the product of a theory such as Marxism. It contains an insight which was all too rare among self-styled liberals who saw totalitarianism, if they really saw it, in Nazi Germany or Fascist Italy or Imperial Japan, but were not capable of discerning it in the Soviet Union, their perpetual blind spot.

Another uncommon insight was evident in Dewey's remark that "neither theory nor practical experience has as yet shown that state socialism will be essentially different from state capitalism." [219] This statement seems to imply that, as of 1939 at least, Soviet Russia had not attained the status of a Socialist, let alone a Communist, state—contrary to the popular impression. It seemed to forecast the difficulty, if not indeed the impossibility, of the attainment of communism by the Soviet Union in the forseeable future. Realistic and honest citizens of the Soviet will admit that communism is still a long way ahead and that there are deep differences in income, social status, and comforts among the various occupational, political, and ethnic levels in the U. S. S. R. However, Communist party members and sympathizers will insist, as they did to me in 1960, that communism is inevitable in their country and eventually everywhere. Some hold to such a viewpoint with the tenacity of a religious person to a theological tradition.

The year *Freedom and Culture* appeared was also the date of the publication of a compilation of papers about Dewey's thought, *The Philosophy of John Dewey*. In his commentary upon the essays of the various contributors, Dewey included some sentences on the question which probably occupied the center of his work and thought. According to the eighty-year-old philosopher, ". . . the idea that the revolution in its immediate occurrence, as of a given date, 1789 or 1917/18, is anything more than the beginning of a gradual process is a case of Utopian self-delusion. The method of intelligent action has to be applied at every step of that process in which a revolution 'runs its course.' Its final outcome does not depend upon the original abrupt revolutionary occurrence but upon the way intelligent action intervenes at each step of its course—as all history shows in spite of *ex post facto* 'inevitabilities' constructed *after* choice has manifested its effects. Perhaps the worst feature of social philosophies that substitute inevitabilities, materialistic in nature, for choices moral in nature because made after intelligent evaluation, is not that they get rid of choice, but that by eliminating intelligent valuation they put a premium on arbitrary choice." [220] The way of the democratic, evolutionary society is thus sharply contrasted with that of the revolutionary (*i.e.,* Communistic) society, and there is no doubt as to which is superior.

This contrast should be fully appreciated, Dewey felt, in the free societies. As he wrote later in the same essay, ". . . we may felicitate ourselves that we live where free discussion and free criticism are still values which are not denied us by some power reaching out for a monopoly of cultural and spiritual life. The inability of human beings in so many parts of the world to engage in free exchange of ideas should make us aware, by force of contrast, of the privilege we still enjoy and of our duty of defending and extending it. It should make us aware that free thought itself, free inquiry, is crippled and finally paralyzed by suppression of free communication. Such communication includes the right and responsibility of submitting every idea and every belief to severest criticism. It is less important that we all believe alike than that we all alike inquire freely and put at the disposal of one another such glimpses as we may obtain of the truth for which we are in search." [221] Dewey's standard "of submitting every idea and every belief to severest criticism" seems to reflect, to some extent at least, the quality of an absolute. Did Dewey really mean *every* idea? There is little evidence that Dewey subjected to the "severest criticism" his earlier impressions and views concerning the U. S. S. R.

Some writers, like Sidney Hook, have found general similarities between the philosophical viewpoint of John Dewey and that of Karl Marx. Jim Cork, an American Marxist who also found much to admire in John Dewey, cited nine areas of agreement between Marx and Dewey, which he regarded as "sufficient to warrant investigation into a possible ideological rapprochement between the philosophical outlooks of these two influential figures." [222] This was a possibility which Cork could entertain because he "had always thought of Dewey as a left-wing Jeffersonian democrat with socialist tendencies." [223] However, Cork was by no means happy with Dewey's approach to Marxism. Even though he discussed Marx and his ideas at greater length in *Freedom and Culture* than elsewhere in his writings, he dispensed with his "usual scientific caution and genial objectivity" in evaluating Marxism, contended Cork, who also complained that Dewey did not show a "first-hand knowledge of Marx's writings" and did not "distinguish between Marx's own ideas and encrustations upon them of subsequent interpretations. . . ." [224] Above all, Cork could not understand "why Dewey has so signally failed to distinguish between Marx's ideas and morals and those of Stalinists. He seems to have been unduly influenced by the latters' tiresome claim that they were the only legitimate descendants of Marx." [225]

It is difficult to believe that Dewey did not read the writings of Marx with care. However, to judge from the fact that Marx and Marxism appear in Dewey's writings with relative rareness, it would be too much to argue that Dewey was a Marxist.

Geiger, for example, disposed of the nine parallels between Marx and Dewey adduced by Cork as suffering "in general from the undistributed middle." [226] A historian might use the expression *post hoc non ergo propter hoc* to characterize the general similarity and coincidence of ideas which cannot be accounted for, on the basis of demonstrable documentary or equivalent evidence, that there was some sort of cause-and-effect relationship in ideas between the two men, in spite of their common starting-point in Hegel. Geiger, in fact, maintains that, ". . . except for a period in the 1930's when at least one aspect of Marxism, economic determinism, played a conspicuous part in his writings, Dewey cannot be said to have been a Marxist; and of course his later attacks on Marx were decisive." [227] Randall, too, noted similarities between Marx and Dewey. He pointed to Dewey's debt to Hegel and to the fact that Dewey's philosophical position ". . . owes much also to the left-wing Hegelians like Marx who bent Hegel's idealism of social experience to the active service of changing the world. But the obvious points of contact should not be taken as they have sometimes been, to obscure the essential differences." [228]

DEWEY AND STALINIST COMMUNISM. If there seems to be some doubt as to the real relation of Dewey to Marxism, there can be none about his personal feelings and public statements about Stalinist Communism as practiced in the Soviet Union. As far back as 1932, Hook says, the Kremlin sought to win over Dewey to its cause through the mediation of the American Communist leader, Earl Browder. The Communist Party "realized that it could not capture the liberal movement unless it had John Dewey in tow. So long as he stayed out of its chief fronts or was critical, the hegemony of the Communist party over large sections of American liberal opinion was incomplete or threatened." [229] But Dewey refused to be taken in, either by flattery, offers of trips, threats, denunciations, and even the possibility of character assassination.

Dewey always remained a thorn in the side of the Communists even when they were getting a sympathetic hearing in wider circles, as during World War II. An example of this was the letter to the *New York Times* by Dewey in January, 1942.

Dewey recalled that "Stalin, now in the Allied camp by Hitler's will, not his, unleashed the present war through his pact with Hitler" and warned that "Stalin's actions—and those of his agents and sympathizers here—will be governed by his own interest as he conceives it, regardless of the efforts or the consequences to his present democratic allies. . . ."[230] After presenting some details to buttress his suspicion of Stalin and his foreign agents and sympathizers, Dewey concluded that "our future would be much more secure than it now appears if we were to emulate his [Stalin's] circumspection instead of indulging in the fatuous one-sided love feast now going on in this country."[231] Again, as in the case of his prediction that Hitler and Stalin would become allies, Dewey saw Stalin for what he really was even while he was on the side of the United States in the war against Nazi Germany. He agreed apparently with the maxim of Ovid, "fas est ab hoste doceri," and accordingly felt that it was wrong to have Communist agents and sympathizers in the United States without having democratic agents and sympathizers in the Soviet Union. In other ways, too, such as in his criticism of the wartime film, "Mission to Moscow," Dewey showed that he was not at all deluded by the professions of the Soviet and the American Communists.[232]

I have included this discussion of Dewey's political views because they are important in accounting for the real reason for the Soviet attitude toward John Dewey. What Dewey said and did about Soviet communism influenced the Soviet authorities' opinion of him more than what he had written on education. It will be shown that Dewey the educator was equated with Dewey the citizen and public figure.

Dewey's reputation as an educator suffered considerably in Soviet Russia from the mid-thirties onward. With a few exceptions,[233] his name and his ideas no longer appeared in the educational writings. A full study should be done on references to Dewey in Soviet educational writings from the late thirties until the present. Because much of the significant and pertinent literature is not available, I will analyze only a sampling in this essay (see pp. 113–32); I believe, however, that in a closed society, such as the Soviet Union, the variations in attitude on an important subject will not be fundamental. One might also predict

that open antagonism to American educational thought, and to
Dewey himself, would diminish during the period of World
War II when the United States and the U. S. S. R. were allies.

THE POSTWAR PERIOD: 1945–60. After the end of World
War II in 1945, it might have been expected, furthermore, that
there would be a profound change in the Soviet attitude toward
the West, including America, and the non-Communist ideas and
achievements of those areas.[234] This change was not long in
coming. On August 14, 1946, the Central Committee of the
Communist Party of the Soviet Union passed a resolution "On
the Journals *Zvezda* and *Leningrad;*" on August 26, 1946, "On
the Repertoire of the Dramatic Theatres and Measures for Its
Improvement;" and on September 4, 1946, "On the Moving
Picture *Bolshaia Zhizn.*" Finally, on February 10, 1948, the
Central Committee handed down a resolution "On the Opera
Velikaia Druzhba by V. Muradeli." After the first resolution,
on August 21, 1946, Andrei A. Zhdanov, the new intellectual
and cultural dictator of the U. S. S. R., delivered an interpretative address concerning that resolution to the First All-Union
Congress of Soviet Writers. The resolutions, together with the
address by Zhdanov, became the "authoritative guide in the
shaping of policy and practice in all departments of the cultural
apparatus."[235] In this way began the complete control of Soviet
cultural life in line with the principle of "Zhdanovshchina," that
is, the elevation of Soviet values, together with the total exclu-
sion of foreign—including American—cultural and intellectual
influences from Soviet life.

It was inevitable that the educational leaders would respond
to the new call for cultural conformity. At a general meeting in
Moscow, October 19, 1946, professors and others engaged in
higher education decided unanimously to send a letter to "our
wise leader and teacher, the greatest scholar of our epoch—
Joseph Vissarionovich Stalin!" pledging complete co-operation.
The directives of the Central Committee, said the Moscow
professors, ". . . oblige us to strengthen the ideological work,
tirelessly to nurture our youth in the spirit of cheerfulness and
of faith in our cause, in the spirit of devotion to the socialist
Motherland, competent and able to overcome difficulties.

"In instructing and educating our youth we do not forget for a moment that every science is a Party science and that its teaching cannot be separated from the politics of the Party. That politics is the vital base of the Soviet political order.

"We, professors and instructors, obligate ourselves so to conduct our work that every day spent by a student in a higher educational institution will nurture in him Bolshevik ideology, broaden his political and cultural horizon, and enrich him with the knowledges of his specialty." [236] What would happen next to the reputations of foreign educators, including John Dewey, could be accurately predicted.

The Academy of Pedagogical Sciences of the R. S. F. S. R. played a leading role in the application of the new cultural Party line to education. President Ivan A. Kairov had indeed taken the initiative from the Moscow professors when, on October 11, 1946, more than a week before their letter to Stalin, he told the members of the Academy that "the Central Committee of the Party demands that all workers on the ideological front, and consequently workers in pedagogical science, understand that they are placed in the advanced line of fire." [237] The official and scholarly periodical of the Academy, *Sovetskaya Pedagogika,* carried an editorial on the Central Committee resolutions as early as the issue of October–November, 1946. Entitled "For Bolshevik Ideology in Soviet Pedagogical Science," the editorial confessed that "the serious shortcomings exposed recently by the Central Committee on the ideological front are unquestionably present in our pedagogical sciences" and stated firmly that "we must not forget for a moment that every science is Party science" and that ". . . teaching cannot be divorced from the politics of Party and state." [238] The obvious conclusion was that "workers in pedagogical science must first of all study stubbornly, persistently, and consistently the sciences—the Marxist-Leninist theory" and that they ". . . must become bold and militant propagandists of the great Communist ideas of educating the new man." [239] The reader will note the 100 per cent agreement between the Soviet academic professors and educationists that "every science is Party science."

Subsequent issues of *Sovetskaya Pedagogika* offered details on how to apply the Central Committee's ukases to specific school subjects. For example, "in comparing the U. S. S. R. with capitalist countries," the teacher should indicate ". . . the superiority of socialist over capitalist economy" and the fact ". . . that the U. S. S. R. is certain to develop much more rapidly than any capitalist country, including the United States of America." [240] The teacher of literature was directed to inculcate the idea that ". . . love for the socialist Motherland in Soviet people is joined with burning hatred toward her enemies," [241] in accordance with the viewpoint of Stalin. The teacher of the history of education was required to paint a ". . . much clearer picture of the *latest contemporary bourgeois pedagogy*" and to show that "the majority of the representatives of contemporary West-European and American educational theory actually serve reactionary political purposes under a mask of 'objectivity,' 'scientific approach,' and 'love for the child.'" [242] The article goes on to emphasize that the ". . . rôle of Dewey is very significant in this connection." [243] These quotations can be multiplied by reference to this and other periodicals written for the Soviet educational profession.

The cold war was now definitely extended to the realm of educational theory. The knives were being gradually sharpened for the attack on Dewey and the other non-Soviet educators who had had an impact or might possibly have one on education in the U. S. S. R. The Academy of Pedagogical Sciences was not the only source of opposition to Western ideas on education. The All-Union Society for the Dissemination of Political and Scientific Knowledge, which was founded in June, 1947, to carry on propaganda in behalf of the Party line in cultural affairs, was also concerned with thought control in the field of education. On October 24, 1947, Academician A. G. Kalashnikov, Minister of Education of the R. S. F. S. R., told the Society in his review of three decades of Soviet education that "The classical works of Lenin and Stalin laid the theoretical foundation of Soviet pedagogy—a new Soviet science of the education of children." [244] All would have been well if educators had contented themselves with these classics and with the works of Soviet educators which were based upon them. "However, during the years 1925–30 deviations from the instructions of Lenin were observed in school practice. The obsequiousness and genuflection on the part of some Soviet educators before the educational theory and practice of Western Europe and America led to the uncritical introduction into the Soviet school of methods of education evolved by reactionary bourgeois pedagogy. This found its expression in the so-called complex programs, the project method, the Dalton Plan, and the laboratory brigade method, which were imposed on Soviet schools." [245] Even though Dewey was not mentioned in the passage, there could be no doubt that he was one of the "reactionary bourgeois" pedagogues who had "imposed" his methods on the unwilling Soviet school system. The term "reactionary bourgeois pedagogy," it should be noted, became the regular epithet which accompanied the name of a Western pedagogue, particularly Dewey.

Professor Kalashnikov moved on to correlate politics with educational theory. "The struggle of the Trotskyist and right-opportunist elements against the general line of the Party during the period found its counterpart in the field of pedagogy. The Party was obliged to conduct a decisive warfare, on the one hand, with the leftist, anti-Leninist 'theory of the withering away of the school,' and, on the other hand, with right-opportunist elements who strove to preserve the remnants of the old scholastic school and disregard the socialist nature of the Soviet school." [246]

In the section of his address entitled "The Degradation of the School and Pedagogy in Bourgeois Countries," Kalashnikov was especially critical of American education and American pedagogues. And here he became the pioneer of Soviet pedagogical criticism of Dewey. According to Kalashnikov, "The anti-democratic and anti-humanistic practice of American schools is in full accord with those pedagogical 'theories' which are widely disseminated in contemporary America and are an expression of the class interests of American imperialists." [247] In the next sentence he supplied an example of what he had in mind. He cited *The Problems of Men,* by Dewey, "the famous American philosopher and educator," whom he charged with attempting to prove that the purpose of the school is to help the child ". . . to become a shrewd 'businessman' [and] . . . to nurture in the younger generation . . . that warlike reaction which is propagated by American imperialists." [248] While Dewey was given a respectful identification by Kalashnikov, it is nonetheless obvious that the Soviet educational leader was depicting Dewey as a warmonger who was the tool and the lackey of American imperialists. This was but a relatively mild form of criticism which developed in later years into downright denunciation.

As Professor George S. Counts has demonstrated, Kalashnikov completely distorted Dewey's educational philosophy; for example, he combined part of a sentence from one of Dewey's essays with a statement of his own, thus making the American support "those things against which he has always fought," a procedure which shows "a disregard for truth that is utterly frightening. . . ." [249] According to Counts, Kalashnikov's misuse of another American educator's article "reveals the Communist technique of deliberately perverting truth." [250] As a matter of fact, "The minister of education knew that his references were false, but as a good 'Party man' he 'lashed out boldly' at bourgeois education in obedience to the command of Zhdanov and the Central Committee. . . . Whether the 'Party writer' selects truth or falsehood depends on which he thinks is the 'sharper weapon' at the moment." [251]

It is pertinent to point out, in support of Counts' analysis of the methodology of Kalashnikov in pedagogical controversy, that in the 1920's this Soviet educator was a proponent of the Progressive practices which he condemned in 1947. After the decree in 1931 by the Central Committee of the Communist Party which discontinued the activity school, Kalashnikov "disappeared from the educational scene" and "reappeared" only after World War II,[252] ostensibly after he had fully purged himself of pernicious pedagogical principles or "errors." It is highly probable that Kalashnikov's zeal in fighting the enemy doctrines stemmed from his natural desire to prove himself "kommunistischer als Stalin," to paraphrase a well-known expression.

The campaign against Dewey was taken up by Soviet philosophers, who accused him of "American idealistic obscurantism," of exalting "atomic-dollar 'democracy,'" and of "hatred toward the masses." [253] Apparently, there was a sort of competition in the late 1940's and early 1950's among Soviet intellectuals to see who could throw the strongest adjectives at Dewey.

Professor Vladimir A. Veikshan, the leading Soviet specialist in comparative education and in Tolstoi's pedagogy, stated in 1948 that pragmatism has "one of its most prominent representatives in the reactionary philosopher and pedagogue, Dewey," whose philosophy ". . . deprecates the role of children's personal experience, propagates petty busy-work in methods of instruction, propagandizes the project method, nurtures in children a hostile attitude toward true democracy, etc." [254] I am personally acquainted with Veikshan, who has always been moderately critical of Dewey, but on pedagogical rather than political grounds. However, Veikshan has never been a typical Soviet critic of Dewey.

In an article paralleling that of Kalashnikov, Professor Nikolai A. Konstantinov, Academician of Pedagogical Sciences, chairman of the department of pedagogy at the University of Moscow, and noted educational historian, contented himself in 1948 with a passing reference to the influence of Dewey's bourgeois pedagogy upon Blonskii's "Trudovaya Shkola" (1919).[255] Also in a moderately critical vein were the sentences concerning Dewey and the pragmatists in a pamphlet issued in 1948 by the Soviet military director of education for Brandenburg in the Soviet Zone of Germany.[256] The Russian educator characterized the Dewey approach to didactics as "false," but made no attempt at vilification. A third brief critical but nonpolitical comment on Dewey was included in 1948 by Medinskii in an historical essay. This well-known Soviet educator, discussing the period 1921–29, referred to the destructive influence of the project method of the "American reactionary ideology-pedagogues John Dewey, Collings, and Kilpatrick." [257]

Early in the year 1949, the Soviet authorities inaugurated a "campaign of hate against America" and the newspapers at once made a strenuous effort, "without the slightest regard for facts," to eradicate "from the minds of the Soviet people, and particularly the youth, the last vestige of friendly feeling toward their wartime ally." [258] This was the time when the Soviet power made a direct assault on Jewish intellectuals, whom it charged with the crime of "cosmopolitanism." Moreover, in connection with this intensification of the cultural control of the country, the Central Committee of the Communist Party decided to incorporate the spirit of the ideological decisions in a revised

edition of the *Bolshaya Sovetskaya Entsiklopediya.* The new
edition, in the words of *Pravda,* "must show with conviction
and in full the superiority of socialist culture over the decadent
culture of the capitalist world" and "proceeding from the
Marxist-Leninist theory . . . must expose imperialist aggression
and apply Party criticism to contemporary bourgeois movements in the realms of science, technology, and culture" and
"must be saturated with the Bolshevik Party spirit." [259] The
results of the revision were seen in the articles on the sensitive
subjects, including the one on John Dewey.

One of the products of the cold war in pedagogical theory
was an article, "The School and Pedagogy in the U. S. A. in the
Service of Reaction," published in the November, 1949, issue
of *Sovetskaya Pedagogika,* by Professor Nikolai K. Goncharov.
This Soviet expert, now first vice-president of the Academy of
Pedagogical Sciences and editor of *Sovetskaya Pedagogika,* is
also the co-author of *Pedagogika,* a textbook on Soviet educational principles which has played an influential role, especially
since the publication of the 1946 edition, in the training of
Soviet teachers. In 1947, George S. Counts and Nucia P. Lodge
translated a section of this volume under the title *I Want to Be
Like Stalin.*

After attacking various aspects of American education in
"The School and Pedagogy in the U. S. A. in the Service of Reaction" Goncharov presented his main point—that education
in the United States is not democratic, but rather "reactionary"
and that this is due to the fact that "American reactionary
pedagogy provides the 'theoretical foundations' of reactionary
educational practice in the schools of the U. S. A." [260] The
"reactionary American educators strive to show their loyalty to
the masters of Wall Street by building the theoretical foundations of the American system of education." [261] Included in this
group are such "hardened bison as the 90-year-old John Dewey,"
Counts, William McGucken, Kilpatrick, and others who have
set aside their philosophical differences and formed a united
educational front, since "they all experience an animal fear of
the crisis of the capitalist system and strive to find the most skillful and subtle ways of stupefying the toiling masses." [262] Those
who take Soviet educational scholarship at face value should

note the mode of thought and expression of this leading exponent of Soviet pedagogical science. The presumed educational
scientist writing in a scholarly journal which is the organ of the
Academy of Pedagogical Sciences did not make even a token
effort to provide documentary support for his conclusion that
American educators were tools of Wall Street. It would be far
easier to demonstrate that Professor Goncharov was striving to
show his loyalty to the one and only master of the Kremlin.

Any attempt to read logic into Goncharov's critique of Dewey
is futile. Dewey and Counts were labeled as "ideological armor-
bearers of American imperialism." [263] According to Goncharov,
Dewey's call to the schools to teach children and youth how to
think independently in the face of the newspaper and radio
propaganda, was "designed to confuse the American people on
the question of the true role of the school. The hypocritical
professions of Dewey about the duties of the school constitute an
attempt to disguise the corrupting influence of the American
school upon the growing generation.

"Dewey is forced to admit that youth in the U. S. A. have no
opportunity to apply their powers. The capitalist system of
economy, with its anarchy of production, breeds crises and un-
employment. However, Dewey's criticism of this system is
designed to preserve and strengthen the existing capitalist
order." [264] In Dewey's criticism that the contemporary education
system lacked a basic aim or inspiring social idea, he merely
"plays the simpleton," since the American system has an "idea"
which "so clearly expresses the interests of monopoly capital
that Dewey strives to veil it." [265] Throughout his article
Goncharov used such phraseology as "reactionary," "animal
fear," "cloudy thought," and the like so frequently that it would
be tedious to quote much of it. One more typical quotation
about Dewey's capitalist outlook will suffice. "Dewey is mortally
afraid of the wrath of the people. As a true servant of the
plutocrats, he is terrified lest the toilers establish a social order
devoted to the interests of the people. Therefore he advocates
that education be employed to perfect capitalist relations and
the exploitation of man by man." [266]

From capitalism Goncharov went on to the subject of war.
"Counts, Dewey, and others belong entirely among the most

frantic expansionists and instigators of war. They shout louder than their masters about the necessity of extending the influence of the U. S. A. throughout the world and of carrying the American system of education into all corners of the globe." [267] Again, the pedagogical scientist of the Soviet Union comes to his conclusion on the basis of imaginative interpretation rather than direct documentary evidence.

The next item of criticism concerned the characterization by "American reactionary educators" of Soviet patriotic education as nationalistic. According to Goncharov, Counts, Dewey, and others "preach cosmopolitanism, pour buckets of mud and slander on our school and on the schools of the countries of people's democracy because they cultivate in the young love for the motherland." [268] Since the best form of defense is considered to be an attack, Goncharov turned the charge around and stated that "the reactionaries are putting into practice a genuinely nationalistic and racist education." [269] The language used by Goncharov is more reminiscent of the street than of the seminar: "spat upon by reactionary educators," "howling," and the like. This was doubtless deemed a defensible use of the language in debate because Goncharov was employing all possible methods to discredit those American educators who, he believed, were traitors to humanity by reason of their "ideological preparation for war."

Goncharov explained the opposition of Counts and Dewey to Soviet patriotic education on the ground of the conspiracy against "the national independence of certain countries" inherent in the Marshall Plan. Dewey and Counts, "American reactionary educators" that they were, "have joined this game. Under the guise of new 'discoveries' in educational science they attempt to drag in reactionary cosmopolitan junk and thus aid the American monopolists in the realization of their imperialist policy." [270]

Finally, "Dewey, Counts, Kilpatrick and other ideologists of American reaction, by pouring dirty slander over communism, the most advanced and progressive theory, attempt to present to the American people a distorted picture of the system of education in the U. S. S. R. which is a genuinely democratic and a genuinely humane system."

"Dewey, Counts and other educational theorists like them wage a most decisive struggle for the preservation of the bourgeois influence not only in economics but in ideology as well. They place pedagogy wholly in the service of the political interests of American reactionaries." [271] In Goncharov's concluding sentences, consisting of comments on a quotation by Lenin concerning "bourgeois professors," there are such picturesque phrases as "professors of atomic pedagogy" and "the rabid activity the bourgeoisie and their learned churls develop in our times. . . ." [272] He kept in character to the end.

Professor Counts followed each translated passage by Goncharov with his own refutation by reference to the American sources which the Russian educator cited. According to Counts, "The reader will also note Goncharov's impressive parade of scholarship—his numerous citations of and quotations from American educational literature." [273] This article, which is "typical of Soviet scholarship . . . is the inevitable expression of the ethics of totalitarianism in the realm of things of the mind . . . clearly reminiscent of the writings of the defenders and protagonists of the Nazi regime." [274] Goncharov's "many . . . distortions assume the form of outright and apparently deliberate fabrications" and "cannot be explained in terms of simple ignorance," mainly because ". . . Goncharov is merely responding as a 'loyal soldier' to the command of his superiors in the Communist hierarchy, the Central Committee of the All-Union Communist Party." [275]

In his concluding paragraph, Counts reminded his readers that Goncharov's critique was ". . . not the article of a free man or an independent scholar," but rather ". . . an expression of the policy of the Soviet state from which no deviation is tolerated." [276] The Goncharov article, Counts stated, was only one among "a hundred" of a similar pattern in *Sovetskaya Pedagogika*. This would indicate, reasoned Counts, that "in the Soviet Union falsification, like everything else, is monolithic. All who speak or write must tell the same lie. This means that behind the 'iron curtain' even scholarship, the last hope of truth, has become a naked political weapon. In its historic sense, therefore, scholarship is dead." [277]

In a later work, Counts described the Goncharov article as

follows: "Goncharov makes an impressive parade of scholarship with forty citations and quotations from American journals and educational literature. The uninitiated and uninformed Russian teacher or citizen could only conclude that the picture presented is wholly accurate and trustworthy. Yet a careful checking of the author's citations and quotations, some of them quite extended, shows that he had not the slightest hesitation in completely distorting the facts. The article as a whole is a tissue of fabrications. He would even remove or insert a negative to prove his basic thesis—that all schools and educators in the United States were serving the cause of the 'American monopolists' bent on world conquest and domination. Such is scholarship in the service of the cause of Marx and Lenin." [278]

It will be noted that Goncharov coupled Counts with Dewey, even placing the former's name first on several occasions. This may have been a response to Counts and Lodge's translation of part of his and Yesipov's *Pedagogika* as *I Want to Be Like Stalin*,[279] to which Counts had added a long interpretative introduction. I heard Professor Goncharov lash out bitterly against Counts at a conference of the heads of the departments of the Academy of Pedagogical Sciences and two American professors on December 23, 1957, in Moscow. Professor Goncharov said that he knew the writings of Counts and that he must be incompetent because of his ignorance of the Russian language. In response to this charge, I testified that I had heard Professor Counts translate orally column after column of *Pravda,* chosen from the ceiling-high stacks in his office.

As one reads Counts' refutation of the allegations made by Goncharov, it is easy to see that he returns blow for blow. Although he does not descend to the depths of language where Goncharov prefers to dwell, at times Counts uses sweeping terminology which is out of place in a scientific dissection of another man's errors. In view of the evidence adduced by Counts "fabrication" and similar expressions may seem appropriate; however, it would be more accurate and just to qualify conclusions imputing deliberate falsification to a writer, regardless of nationality. Intent must be established beyond doubt, whether in a court of law or in a court of scholarship. The case would be strengthened if source materials were interpreted with great strictness and verbal restraint. To quote a Communist calumny is to condemn it. If this caution is not observed, one adds ammunition to the arsenal of his adversary.

Another observation about Goncharov is relevant. He was apparently reacting to Dewey's outspoken criticism of Stalinist Communism after the Trotsky investigation, as well as to other critical expressions by Dewey regarding the Soviet Union. If he had not overlooked Dewey's generally favorable report on Soviet education of 1928 he could not have charged Dewey with presenting "a distorted picture" of the Soviet education system and with pouring "buckets of mud and slander" on the schools of the Soviet Union and of the "people's democracies." Goncharov could have attacked Dewey on an earlier occasion, but he waited until the crackdown on American friendship in 1949.

The comment on Dewey in the 1950 edition of the Yesipov-Goncharov *Pedagogika* is rather mild by comparison with Goncharov's remarks in the *Sovetskaya Pedagogika* article. Dewey and his followers, according to this book, "are developing a program of educating youth in the spirit of private property morality which justifies the plundering profits of capitalism. . . ."[280]

The second edition of the *Large Soviet Encyclopedia* carried a brief article on John Dewey which represented unquestionably the fruits of the campaign of hatred toward the United States. John Dewey was described as "a reactionary bourgeois philosopher and sociologist . . . ideologically serving the interests of aggressive American imperialism" and as one who believes that "any view or fanciful notion which profits and pleases American imperialists, can be proclaimed 'scientific' and 'true' with the help of this 'philosophy.' "[281] Moreover, "Dewey attempts to disguise the reactionary character of his sociology and his intentional defense of the piratical imperialistic state by the hypocritical use of the phraseology of liberalism and by a deceitful 'criticism' of the most obvious vices of capitalism. In the interests of the aggressive policy of the government of the U. S. A., Dewey fights with all his resources against the principles of national sovereignty, and actively preaches the co-operation of the classes and the rejection of what he calls 'irrational' class struggle. . . . Propagating racial prejudice, amoralism, unscrupulousness, Dewey cynically proposes that moral norms be replaced by 'working plans of action' adapted to situations that arise. For the bourgeoisie and their governmental workers, according to Dewey, any means are good which fortify the position of capitalism and prevent social revolution. In education, Dewey is a supporter of those methods of instruction which contribute to the rearing of energetic and enterprising defenders of capitalism who are permeated with a spirit of worship of capital and hatred toward communism." [282]

This enlightening article, which was reduced to about two-thirds of a column from the longer and more complimentary article in the 1931 edition, concludes with the statement that, "the philosophy of Dewey is a philosophy of war and fascism. Dewey is the mouthpiece of modern imperialistic reaction, the ideologist of American imperialism, a violent enemy of the U. S. S. R., the countries of the People's Democracy, and the revolutionary theory of Marxism-Leninism." [283] According to Professor Levit, who translated this article from the Russian, "the implications here of the deteriorating possibilities of intercultural communication are horrendous." [284] It might be added that the encyclopedia article seemed to be an echo of the style of Professor Goncharov, and was typical of the Soviet attitude —general and pedagogical—toward Dewey.

The publication of the article on Dewey in the *Bolshaya Sovetskaya Entsiklopediya* during the year of John Dewey's death may have been a coincidence, as may have been the 143-page study by Professor V. S. Shevkin of *The Pedagogy of J. Dewey in the Service of Contemporary American Reaction,* under the imprint of the publishing house of the Ministry of Education of the R. S. F. S. R. This book, incidentally, was recommended by Professor Vladimir A. Veikshan, then the head of the section on comparative education of the Academy of Pedagogical Sciences, to the members of the Comparative Education Society who had a conference with him on September 9, 1958, in Moscow. Professor Veikshan told me at that time that the Shevkin study represented the best example of recent research on the history of educational theory by a Soviet expert. I was fortunate enough to obtain in a bookstore, immediately after the conference, what was probably the last remaining copy of this paperbound book—in a torn condition—for two and a half rubles. It proved valuable for getting an insight into Soviet scholarship in the realm of educational philosophy.

The volume has five chapters, the first of which is entitled "Two Worlds and Two Pedagogues." (Since it is not feasible to include a thoroughgoing review in this essay, the contents will only be outlined in detail.) The two worlds which are contrasted are the capitalist and the socialist, together with their corresponding theories of education, the bourgeois and the Soviet. The chapter's concluding section maintains that "Contemporary bourgeois pedagogy is the enemy of the people, of democracy, and of progress." [285] In this way Shevkin summed up the entire non-Communist philosophy of education.

It is interesting to note that Dewey first appears on page 22 of this 30-page chapter and is not mentioned again until the last three pages. There is scattered mention of such foreign educators as Comenius, Rousseau, Pestalozzi, Herbart, Froebel, and Spencer, and also brief discussions of Russian and Soviet educators, e.g., Belinskii, Hertsen, Dobroliubov, Chernishevskii, Ushinskii, Krupskaya, Kalinin, and Makarenko. The "educators" whose ideas are given most attention are Marx and Engels, Lenin, and Stalin. In point of actual fact, of the thirty-three footnotes in this chapter, fourteen are to Lenin's writings, nine to those of Marx and Engels (collectively and individually), four to Stalin's, two to A. A. Zhdanov's, and one each to the works of Kalinin, Malenkov, and even Herbart, with one reference to the programs of the Communist Party. Not one citation is made to the many writings of Dewey, who is supposed to be the subject of this monograph.

Dewey is first mentioned in the book by Shevkin when the author criticizes him and Thorndike as "reactionary American pedagogues" whose theory recognizes "the immutability of innate human nature." [286] The second time his name occurs is in the context of an attack upon teaching the idea of One World to young people. Shevkin's phraseology represents an interesting approach to scientific argumentation: "Such wicked enemies of science as Dewey and Kilpatrick, have already publicized for a long time their pragmatist pedagogy as a world pedagogic system. . . ." [287] The third reference is concerned with the identi-

fication of John Dewey as the head of the most widespread pedagogical movement in the United States, pragmatism, and as "one
of the leaders of contemporary world ideological reaction." [288]
The other three mentions of Dewey on the last page of the first
chapter deal with the capitalistic nature of Dewey's pedagogy
and are hardly more edifying than the sentences already quoted.

Chapter II, the longest in the book, is entitled "Pragmatism-
Instrumentalism—The Philosophical Foundation of Dewey's
Reactionary Pedagogy." Shevkin presents, in the main, a critical
analysis of the philosophical positions of William James and
John Dewey and actually quotes from their writings; however
most of the citations in the chapter are from the works of Lenin,
Stalin, Marx and Engels, and others with whose thinking the
Communists agree. Not only does Shevkin criticize pragmatism,
but he also joins with pragmatism as "very reactionary philosophies," the schools of personalism, neo-realism, critical realism,
and others. "The representatives of all these schools carry on a
fierce war against the materialist doctrine." [289] Dewey is depicted
as an enemy of true scientific thinking. "The perpetually hypocritical phrases of Dewey about the relationship of ideas and life,
concerning the testing of theory in practice, which he relies upon
to create for the reader a semblance of proof of his false views,
are profoundly inimical to science." [290] Later on, Shevkin rein-
forces this charge by an analysis of "the essence of Dewey's pseu-
doscientific sociology." [291] Still later in the chapter, the Soviet
educational expert confers upon Dewey such titles as a "thorough enemy of science," a spreader of "obscurantism," a justifier
of "imperialist barbarism," "the henchman of contemporary
world imperialist reaction," and one whose thoughts are solely
directed toward the defense of capitalism. This particular series
ends with the statement that "Dewey is the enemy of the scientific idea of development." [292] In the closing pages of this chapter,
Dewey, "the troubadour of American reaction," is said to be
"infinitely hypocritical" whenever he talks about the reorgani-
zation of society; ". . . this reactionary sociologist, philosopher
and pedagogue is the bitterest enemy of progress." [293] After other
extreme statements about Dewey and the degenerate American
culture, Shevkin concludes Chapter II with the following sentence: ". . . the philosophy and sociology of Dewey serve as the

ideological weapon of American imperialism in the struggle against the camp of peace, socialism, and democracy." [294]

Chapter III, "The Pseudo-Scientific Interpretation of Education in J. Dewey's Pedagogy," begins with a repetition of a complaint made previously in the book that the American educator regards education as the panacea for the social problems and evils of the world, as against, presumably, the method of revolution. For the first time, quotations from Dewey are more numerous than those from the favorite Communist sources. Pavlov and Makarenko are cited as authors of more scientific doctrines than the "theories" of Dewey and Thorndike which cling to the idea of the immutability of human nature and thereby play into the hands of the American capitalistic monopolists. This is proof, to Shevkin, of the reactionary and anti-scientific nature of Dewey's pragmatist approach to pedagogy. In the words of the Soviet scientist in education, "Dewey falsifies the scientific conception of the role of education in the life of society," [295] and "The anti-scientific character" of Dewey's conception of human development was "long ago laid bare by the classics of Marxism-Leninism." [296]

The fourth chapter, "School, Pupil, and Teacher as Represented by Pragmatic Pedagogy," adduces 16 quotations from Dewey, only one from a Russian source, Ushinskii, and none from a Communist writer, although Lenin and Stalin are by no means forgotten. In addition to Dewey, the "fallacious" Project Method and Dalton Plan, as well as other individualistic American educational plans, are also given some attention.[297] The first sentence of this chapter refers once more to Dewey's "pseudo-scientific, pragmatic treatment of the nature of man and of education" and maintains that it is at the bottom of Dewey's "equally false interpretation of the problem of the school." [298] Shevkin's major criticisms of Dewey are that he lowers the educational role of the school through his de-emphasis of subject matter and of the role of the teacher in instruction.[299] Some of his statements sound as if they might have come—and some indeed do—from the pens of leading American critics of Dewey. In this chapter, Shevkin comes close to what may be considered a relatively rational approach to an evaluation of the educational thought of John Dewey. It is noteworthy that the Soviet educator did not quote from Dewey's own critique of his extremist followers, *Experience and Education* (1938).

In the fifth chapter, "J. Dewey—The Henchman of Contemporary Imperialist Reaction," Shevkin once more returns to the technique of direct denunciation. Dewey appears in only five footnotes of the chapter's twenty-five, with seven of the references from Lenin and six from Stalin. The Soviet writer lashes out against racialism and anti-communism in America, proof to him of the lack of freedom there. Consequently, when Dewey praises democratic freedom in the United States, Shevkin does not hesitate to say that the philosopher is guilty of "hypocrisy."[300] Dewey, the "apostle of American reaction," the "apologist for imperialism," seeks to hide the true facts about the class nature of the American school, thereby lulling the workers into believing that they have equality of educational opportunity, whereas Dewey, in fact, facilitates the use of the school for the suppression and exploitation of the masses.[301] The objective of Dewey's pedagogy, says Shevkin, is to make education the tool of American imperialism, which aims to achieve fascism at home and domination over the rest of the world.[302]

In the final paragraph of this chapter, Shevkin repeats his charge against Dewey as the apologist of American imperialism and describes him as follows: "Dewey is not only the wicked enemy of the American people, but also of all the freedom-loving peoples of the entire earth."[303]

The book by Shevkin concludes with a seven-page unnumbered chapter. Here are recapitulated the points made in the body of the report, in the same phraseology, *e.g.,* "Dewey is the herald of shameless imperialist reaction" and "the pedagogy of Dewey is saturated with the vile ideology of cosmopolitanism."[304] The "pseudo-scientific instrumentalist pedagogy of J. Dewey"[305] is the root of American crime and barbarism in Korea. "Dewey is the wicked enemy of the Soviet Union," and his protection of the "Trotskyite gang" was the inspiration for criminal behavior toward the Soviet people.[306] On the final page, Shevkin adds a statement on the preservation of peace made by "the great leader of the Soviet people and of all progressive mankind, J. V. Stalin. . . ."[307]

Were this an ordinary book on pedagogy, a critical analysis

of the volume as a whole would have been justified. For example, one might have pointed to the unhistorical and even antihistorical approach of the author in his exposition of Dewey's educational thought, especially through his ignoring—or ignorance—of *Experience and Education* and other writings in which Dewey expressed his disapproval of extremist tendencies among some of his Progressive disciples. One might also have called attention to the seeming lack of awareness by Shevkin of pedagogues in many countries, Russia included, who held ideas in common with Dewey. Or, comment might have been made on the omission of the history of the Progressive (in the non-Communist sense of the term) educators in Russia and the Soviet Union in the first decade or so after the Revolution. However, as it is obvious that Professor Shevkin wrote mainly from the political point of view, such a documented critique is irrelevant. Certainly, the purpose of the book was the denigration of Dewey, personally as well as professionally. The quotations cited on the foregoing pages constitute ample proof that, to an objective observer, to one who is aware of the prestige and influence of Dewey all over the world, this attempt is a failure. One need not be a devotee of Dewey to acknowledge that Shevkin showed himself in this book to be a full follower of the Soviet Communist line, at least as it was in the early 1950's. Except for a small section which seemed to be founded on disagreement with Dewey's doctrines from a pedagogical standpoint, there is almost nothing in this book that would substantiate Professor Veikshan's statement that it is an outstanding specimen of scientific research in pedagogical theory. It would be necessary to stretch the term "scientific" to the breaking point before it could be applied to Shevkin's work, which would not pass as a research study in any country other than a Communist one. With this work, the reputation of John Dewey in the Soviet Union reached bottom. The circumstances of the publication of Shevkin's book by pedagogical publishing house of the Ministry of Education of the R. S. F. S. R. is an indication, if one were really needed, of the official character of this form of "educational research" in a totalitarian society. There can be no doubt at all that the Communist Party and the Soviet regime stood solidly behind the "scientific study" of Shevkin.

In 1955, a translation of a goodly part of Shevkin's volume appeared in East Germany [308] to enlighten pedagogues directly on the accepted view of Dewey, pragmatism, and Progressive Education. It is significant that the German translation, which appended Dewey quotations in English, omits virtually all the extreme terminology. Possibly, the German publisher feared that the teachers of East Germany, familiar with European Progressive Education and also the doctrines of Dewey, might be repelled by unbridled vocabulary. The translator apparently took great pains to cut out the damaging passages, and even parts of sentences and part of the title—without any indication of the omissions—to make Shevkin's book more palatable to a relatively sophisticated audience.

It is evident that the two and a half decades from the time of Dewey's visit in 1928 to 1952, the date of the publication of Shevkin's book and of Dewey's death, were marked by a complete turnabout in the attitude of Soviet educators to John Dewey. Corliss Lamont, who interprets Soviet life and culture rather favorably, offers an explanation that "unhappily Soviet philosophers have weakened their own case by displaying a formidable ignorance of American philosophy especially in their continued misunderstanding of the American School of Naturalism led by the late John Dewey." [309] At best, this statement tells only a small part of the story.

As in the case of some of the earlier periods covered by this essay, source materials for the years following the death of Stalin in 1953 are scarce. Perhaps the resultant thaw and the change in policy regarding communication with the West led to a relaxation of the official attitude with regard to Dewey. A history of pre school education in post-Revolutionary Russia, issued by the publishing house of the Russian Ministry of Education, carries a mention of Dewey [310] among those—Froebel, Tolstoi, and Stanley Hall—who influenced Louise Shleger's work at the beginning of the century. However, this is not a statement by Professor I. V. Chuvashev, the author, but rather a quotation from the writings of Louise Shleger.

The textbook, *Didactics,* written by Danilov and Yesipov in 1957 under the imprint of the Academy of the Pedagogical Sciences of the R. S. F. S. R., represents quite a contrast with the

Shevkin book. First, there is a sober, page-long discussion of Dewey, who is identified without a word of invective or even a negativistic adjective, but simply as "one of the pillars of pragmatism." Moreover, there are three footnote references to John and Evelyn Dewey's *Schools of Tomorrow* (1922 Russian translation). This unusual treatment ends with the opinion that "it is clear that Dewey's theory of instruction is concerned with narrow practicality in the education of youth." [311]

Among the 1958 pedagogical writings, there are several books with references to Dewey. Cherepanov's monograph on Shatskii includes the latter's autobiographical essay, "Moi pedagogicheskii put" ("My Pedagogical Path") in which he expressed his early indebtedness to the ideas of Dewey. [312] An edition of Shatskii's selected pedagogical writings, produced under the aegis of the Academy of Pedagogical Sciences and published in 1958 by the Ministry of Education of the R. S. F. S. R., omits, without any indication of such omission, Shatskii's two paragraphs in his autobiography on the foreign educators (including Dewey and Stanley Hall) from whom he drew pedagogical inspiration. However, it does include Shatskii's neutral sentence referring to Dewey. [313] Also mentioning Dewey in a casual, objective way was the extensive study by Korolev on education during the first three years of Soviet history. [314]

During his many discussions with the members of the Comparative Education Society in Moscow in 1958, Professor Vladimir A. Veikshan was frequently asked about Soviet knowledge of and interest in John Dewey. According to him, "Dewey is studied very deeply" in the Soviet Union. He traced the outline of the influence of Dewey's ideas on Soviet education and explained the decline of interest in Dewey in terms of too wide an application and the lowering of academic achievement. Veikshan felt that there were basic errors in the doctrines of Dewey, mainly the neglect of factual knowledge, which could not be attributed simply to distortions by disciples of Dewey. At no time did he change the approach to Dewey from the professional to the political, as others have done. Perhaps he was especially careful out of consideration for the American guests —a form of professional *mir i druzhba* ("peace and friendship"). In any event, Professor Veikshan talked in a similar vein to members of the 1960 delegation of the Comparative Education Society in Moscow, even though the atmosphere at that time was more highly charged with tension toward the United States. What Professor Veikshan did not mention, either in 1958 or 1960, was the publication in 1958 of Paul C. Crosser's *Nihilizm Dzhona Diyui,* a translation of *The Nihilism of John Dewey* (New York: Philosophical Library, 1955). This was a significant event, because it was the first time that a foreign book on Dewey had been translated into Russian. As a matter of fact, as far as I can determine, it was the fourth Russian book on Dewey, the first two being by Komarovskii (1926, 1930) and the third by Shevkin (1952).

It is interesting to speculate on the reasons Soviet educators published a translation of Crosser's book after having neglected the non-Soviet literature on Dewey for so long. One reason is suggested by the content of the volume, which presents a severe criticism of Dewey's views on science, art, and education. Crosser sums up his attitude to "Dewey's destructive philosophy" by stating that "Dewey has made America lose its perspective and has thus greatly weakened the intellectual potential of American leadership at home and abroad," and by referring to "the utter meaninglessness of Dewey's philosophy of science, the utter emptiness of his philosophy of art, and the utter sterility of his philosophy of education" (Preface, p. ix). Crosser does include two or three sentences of appreciation for Dewey's services to American philosophy, but the book is critical throughout. This may account, in part at least, for Soviet interest in Crosser's work.

A glance through recent and current Soviet pedagogical literature will reveal the absence of Dewey's name where it might ordinarily be expected. A study in 1959 on education from 1921–25, for example, discusses the Dalton Plan, but includes nothing on Dewey.[315] Nor is Dewey mentioned in any of the articles of the issue of *Sovetskaya Pedagogika* commemorating the fortieth anniversary of Soviet education since the October Revolution. Professor N. K. Goncharov severely criticized Professor George S. Counts in a page and a half, but ignored Dewey.[316] The 1955 edition of the textbook on the history of pedagogy edited by Madame M. F. Shabaeva for the Academy of Pedagogical

Sciences, refers briefly to Stanley Hall and Thorndike, but does not mention Dewey.[317]

However, it would be incorrect to maintain that Dewey has been forgotten in Soviet pedagogical writings. The collection of articles and speeches by Andrei S. Bubnov, who served as Commissioner of the People's Education (Narkompros) from 1929 to 1937, contains references to Dewey (1931, 1933) [318] and other American educators. The invaluable compilation by the Academy of Pedagogical Sciences of the Soviet literature on the history of education published between 1918 and 1957 lists five post-revolutionary Russian translations of Dewey's educational writings. In addition, it mentions what was written on Dewey by Russians: Komarovskii's dissertation on Dewey and a review of it in a Marxist journal; an article by Shevkin on "The Reactionary Pedagogy of John Dewey" (*Sovetskaya Pedagogika,* December, 1947); and finally Shevkin's book on the American educator published in 1952, already analyzed in detail.[319]

The useful new pedagogical dictionary, also issued by the Academy of Pedagogical Sciences, devotes nearly a page to the life and work of Dewey, who is identified as "reaktsionnii amerikanskii filosof-idealist i pedagog-teoretik." The treatment is factual, in general, but the anonymous author adds the following evaluation: "However, the practical application of his principles exerted a negative influence on the theory and practice of education in the U. S. A. and in other countries." [320] The final paragraph runs true to Soviet tradition. Here the author states that, from the middle of the 1930's onward, Dewey, who occupied himself with the sociological and political aspects of education, perpetrated "a hostile attack on the Soviet Union." [321] The bibliography contains the five Russian translations of Dewey's works, three educational and three philosophical books by Dewey in English, Shevkin's "study" of Dewey, and the Russian translation of *The Nihilism of John Dewey* by P. K. Crosser (sic). A glance at the list of authors at the end of the second volume reveals the name of B. B. Komarovskii of Baku, as well as those of several others, one of whom might have written this article on Dewey.

It would be idle to speculate on the reputation of Dewey in the Soviet Union in the years to come. At least one experienced writer on Soviet affairs, Isaac Deutscher, seems to imply the possibility of a re-evaluation of Dewey's pedagogical views, since they are similar to the current polytechnic emphasis, which goes back historically to Karl Marx and which is being promoted by the Khrushchev educational reform.[322] However, this does not appear likely—and the door should be kept open for every type of surprise—as long as the cold war is in force.

DEWEY IN CHINA. For a brief comparison, it is pertinent to review John Dewey's experience in another Communist country, continental China. Dewey, who had taught many Chinese students at Columbia University, was invited by the Chinese government in 1919 to lecture in Peking after he concluded his series of lectures in Japan. "As the first foreigner invited by Chinese officials to lecture at a Chinese university, Dewey had at this moment an opportunity seldom given any philosopher." [323] The five lectures on philosophy of education which he delivered at the National University of Peking were repeated at other Chinese universities during the following two years. Then the lectures were printed and reprinted several times, and some of his books were translated into Chinese.

One specific outcome of Dewey's lectures at Peking, especially the one on "Social Philosophy and Political Philosophy," was the powerful impression exerted on Ch'en Tu-hsiu (1879–1942). Ch'en was dean of the Faculty of Arts and Letters of the National University of Peking, and, like Hu Shih (1891–1962) Dewey's former student at Columbia University, was an outstanding intellectual leader of the new China. At the time Ch'en heard Dewey, he was well on the way toward Marxism and toward his future role as a major founder and ideologist of the Chinese Communist Party. Yet, the impact of the lectures was such that the attraction of Leninism "was to be delayed by a strong counterinfluence—the social philosophy of John Dewey." [324] However, the delay lasted but two years. Instead of becoming a liberal or social democrat, Ch'en joined Li Ta-Chao (1888–1927) in 1921 as co-founder of the Communist Party of China.[325]

Dewey's major influence in China was in the area of education, and his contribution was "original, decisive, lasting," [326] particularly in educational theory and research. What appealed to the Chinese educators were Dewey's doctrines of education for living, the child-centered class, and the school as a society. Dewey's general achievements as a result of his stay in China might be summed up as follows: successful intellectual communication with the Chinese thinkers, comprehension of the Chinese people's ability to think and act for themselves, and strengthening of the links between the United States and China. "He was in the 20th century, a secularized Matteo Ricci present at the new court of Chinese scholars assembled at the National University of Peking where devotion to Western thought was as intense as was the devotion in earlier centuries to Confucian thought." [327]

But the best intentions and actions by Dewey were not enough to overcome rising opposition on the part of those who clung to the Chinese humanistic tradition in preference to his positivism and pragmatism. When the increasing influence of Communism was added, it is not surprising that Dewey's ideas were replaced by those of Marxism-Leninism-Stalinism. Nor is it surprising that Communist China, proclaimed as the People's Republic of China in 1949, undertook a campaign to cleanse the country of what it characterized as deleterious intellectual influences. In 1951, an attack was inaugurated against Public Enemy Number One in the intellectual world—Dr. Hu Shih, scholar, diplomat, and "Father of the Chinese Renaissance." To a large extent, the severity of the attack was derived from the fact that Hu Shih was a student of Western thought and of John Dewey. [328] No doubt, the Soviet attitude toward the American philosopher-educator played some role in the denunciations of Dewey and his disciples. Fortunately, Hu Shih was safe in Taiwan, having been spirited out of Peking in an airplane sent by Chiang Kai-shek just as the Communists were entering the city.

Also in 1951, the Communists denounced Ch'en Ho-ch'in, professor of education at Nanking Normal College, and a graduate of Teachers College, Columbia University, for having advocated the "reactionary educational theories" of John Dewey and thereby the ideas of American "imperialism." Communist educators continued their criticism of Ch'en and demanded that

"Dewey's insidious influence" on the educational philosophy of China be eliminated. "Ch'en was compelled to admit his errors and to express his new understanding of the class nature of man and the political significance of all educational work." [329]

The campaign against Hu Shih was stepped up during 1955. For example, ten special articles against him appeared in *Jen-min jih-pao* ("People's Daily") alone; three volumes were necessary to reprint subsequently the anti-Hu articles of the press and periodicals. Typical of the tone of the attacks was a statement by Ho Lin, professor of philosophy at the University of Peking and a former colleague of Hu's: "What Hu Shih expounded was the reactionary bourgeois idealism of imperialism, especially the reactionary pragmatism of John Dewey and William James. Therefore, to remove the prevailing malignancy caused by Hu Shih's ideology from our academic world is of major significance to the task of opposing the idealist ideology that serves modern imperialism." [330] The terminological echo from Moscow is all too clear.

CONCLUSION. The history of the reputation of John Dewey in Russia and the Soviet Union has only been sketched in this essay. The high point—Komarovskii's book (1930)—and the low point—Shevkin's attack (1952)—were described in detail, as were outlines of the changing fortunes of Dewey at other times. The information included in these pages is as extensive as any I have seen in the pedagogical literature of several countries. No doubt, there are gaps which can and should be filled, as well as errors which call for correction. I hope there will be an opportunity for even more detailed work on this study, but it is doubtful that further research would change substantially the main points and conclusions of this essay.

John Dewey and his educational doctrines have been celebrated, studied, and applied all over the world. [331] His ideas have been criticized in various countries but he has been respected as a person. In the world behind the Iron Curtain, however, Poland alone seems to show some respect for the American philosopher-pedagogue. In the United States in recent years, there has been considerable criticism in some quarters of his educational influence. Dewey's fame and fortune have had ups and downs in the Soviet Union. But nowhere and never have his name and personal integrity been dragged in the mud as in the land of Lenin, Stalin, and Khrushchev.

The reaction of the Soviet reader to this essay can be anticipated with reasonable accuracy. On the basis of the Soviet educators' denunciations of John Dewey and George S. Counts, similar attacks on my character and motives might be predicted. In fact, one of the senior research workers of the Academy of Pedagogical Sciences has recently applied the traditional technique of Communist denunciation in her "review" of my chapters in *The Changing Soviet School*.[332] For Soviet pedagogues, and for the record as well, let it be known that I am not and have never been a disciple of Dewey. But this fact will probably make no difference to some Soviet writers who are addicted, in Farrell's felicitous phraseology, to the "language of the political gutter and underworld as a proper medium for literary criticism." [333]

POSTSCRIPT. The April, 1962, issue of the monthly Soviet periodical, *Narodnoe Obrazovanie* (*The People's Education*) carried a five-page article, "Nesostoyatelnaya pretenziya Wilyama Brikmana" ("The Unsubstantiated Arguments of William Brickman"). This is a critique by Professor M. Bernshtein of my short essay, "Dewey and Russia," in *John Dewey: Master Educator*. Professor Bernshtein makes accusations of propaganda and distortion which I hope to analyze at a future date. More important, Bernshtein characterizes Dewey's educational ideas as "perfidious" and "anti-democratic," as supporting the capitalistic monopoly on knowledge and education, and as widening the gap between intellectual and physical labor. In addition, he holds Dewey responsible for the shortcomings of American education.

There appears to be no evidence of any objective reconsideration by Soviet educators of Dewey's role in education.

NOTES

INDEX

1. The Civilizational Functions of Philosophy and Education, *John L. Childs*

1. Ralph Barton Perry, *Characteristically American* (New York: Alfred A. Knopf, Inc., 1949), p 50.
2. John Dewey, *Experience and Nature* (Chicago: Open Court Publishing Company, 1925), p. 38.
3. John Dewey, *Philosophy and Civilization* (New York: Minton, Balch & Co., 1931), p. 3.
4. *Ibid.*, pp. 3-4.
5. *Ibid.*, p. 7.
6. *Ibid.*, p. 6.

7. *Ibid.*, p. 7.
8. John Dewey, *A Common Faith* (New Haven: Yale University Press, n. d. [1934]), p. 87.
9. John Dewey, in *The Educational Frontier,* ed. William H. Kilpatrick (New York: D. Appleton-Century Company, 1933), p. 34.
10. *Ibid.*
11. *Ibid.*, p. 288.
12. John Dewey, *Democracy and Education* (New York: The Macmillan Company, 1916), p. 383.

2. John Dewey's Influence on Educational Practice, *Harold R. W. Benjamin*

1. See Henry B. Binns, *A Century of Education: 1808-1908* (London: J. M. Dent & Sons, Ltd., 1908), p. 5.
2. Quoted from the Henry Barnard manuscript collection by Richard K. Morris, "Parnassus on Wheels: a Biographical Sketch of Henry Barnard, 1811-1900," in *Trinity College Library Gazette,*

Number 2 (February, 1955), p. 8.
3. Francis Biddle, *Mr. Justice Holmes* (New York: Charles Scribner's Sons, 1943), p. 162.
4. John Dewey, *Characters and Events* (New York: Henry Holt & Company, Inc., 1929), I, 100.
5. Biddle, *Holmes,* p. 165.
6. Quoted in Dewey, *Characters and Events,* I, 101.

3. John Dewey on Psychology in High Schools, *Arthur E. Lean*

1. The quotations that follow are taken from John Dewey, "Psychology in High-Schools from the Standpoint of the College," *Papers, Michigan Schoolmasters' Club, First Meeting, May 1, 1886* (Lansing, Michigan: H. R. Pattengill, n. d.).
2. Joseph Ratner, *An Introductory Note on the Proceedings of the First Meeting of the Michigan Schoolmasters' Club* (n. p., n. d.).

4. John Dewey and the Genius of American Civilization, George E. Axtelle

1. John Dewey, *Experience and Nature*, 2nd ed. (Chicago: Open Court Publishing Company, 1958), p. 333.

2. *Ibid.*, p. 167.

3. *Ibid.*, p. 138.

4. Alfred North Whitehead, "John Dewey and His Influence," in *The Philosophy of John Dewey*, ed. Paul A. Schilpp, 2nd ed. (New York: Tudor Publishing Company, n. d. [1951]), pp. 477–78.

5. John Dewey, "The Need for a Recovery of Philosophy," *Creative Intelligence: Essays in the Pragmatic Attitude* (New York: Henry Holt and Co., n. d. [1917]), p. 65.

6. Dewey, *Experience and Nature*, p. 325.

7. *Ibid.*, p. 322.

8. John Dewey, *Democracy and Education* (New York: The Macmillan Company, 1916), p. 387.

9. John Dewey, *Philosophy and Civilization* (New York: Minton, Balch & Co., 1931), p. 7.

10. *Ibid.*, p. 8.

11. John Dewey, *The Quest for Certainty* (New York: Minton Balch & Co., 1929), p. 255.

12. Dewey, *Experience and Nature*, p. 145.

13. John Dewey, *Liberalism and Social Action* (New York: G. P. Putnam's Sons, n. d. [1935]), p. 73.

14. *Ibid.*, pp. 58–59.

15. Dewey, *Experience and Nature*, p. 292.

16. *Ibid.*, p. 296.

17. *Ibid.*

18. *Ibid.*, p. 298.

19. John Dewey, *Art as Experience* (New York: Minton, Balch & Co., n. d. [1934]), p. 35.

20. John Dewey, *Human Nature and Conduct* (New York: Henry Holt & Company, 1922), pp. 161–63.

21. Dewey, *Democracy and Education*, pp. 104–105.

22. *Ibid.*, p. 180.

23. *Ibid.*, p. 171.

24. *Ibid.*, p. 170.

5. Soviet Attitudes toward John Dewey as an Educator, William W. Brickman

1. See William W. Brickman, "John Dewey's Foreign Reputation as an Educator," *School and Society*, LXX (October 22, 1949), 257–265; and "John Dewey: Educator of Nations," in *John Dewey: Master Educator*, eds. William W. Brickman and Stanley Lehrer, 2d ed. (New York: Society for the Advancement of Education, 1961), pp. 132–143.

2. John Dewey, *Jak myslimy* (Warsaw: Ksiazka i Wiedza, 1956).

3. For a short essay on this theme, see William W. Brickman, "John Dewey in Russia," *Educational Theory*, X (January, 1960), 83–88. A shorter version appeared in Brickman and Lehrer, *John Dewey: Master Educator*, pp. 144–147.

4. An overview of what Americans wrote about Russia is presented in Anna M. Babey, *Americans in Russia, 1776–1917* (New York: Comet, 1938). See also Wil-

liam W. Brickman, "Some Historical Notes on Russian-American Relations in Culture and Education," *History of Education Journal*, X (1959), 100–102.

5. William W. Brickman, *The Changing Soviet School*, eds. George Z. F. Bereday, William W. Brickman, and Gerald H. Read (Boston: Houghton Mifflin, 1960), p. 45.

6. Quoted in Raymond Walters, "Is Soviet Education Borrowing from the U. S.?" *School and Society*, LXXXVII (May 9, 1959), 217.

7. For the text, see *French Liberalism and Education in the Eighteenth Century*, F. de la Fontainerie, ed. (New York: McGraw-Hill, 1932), pp. 199–310.

8. L. N. Tolstoi, *Pedagogicheskie sochineniya*, ed. V. A. Veikshan, 2d ed. (Moscow: Uchpedgiz, 1953), p. 214.

9. Jane Addams, *Twenty Years at Hull House* (New York: Macmillan, 1920), p. 280.

10. "The Russia I Believe In," *The Memoirs of Samuel Harper*, ed. Paul V. Harper (Chicago: University of Chicago Press, 1945), pp. 6–7.

11. Salomon M. Teitelbaum, "Progressive Education in the U. S. S. R.," *Journal of Educational Sociology*, XX (February, 1947), 357.

12. *Cf.*, Thomas Woody, *New Minds: New Men?* (New York: Macmillan, 1932), pp. 39, 47; and I. L. Kandel, "John Dewey's Influence on Education in Foreign Lands," *John Dewey: The Man and His Philosophy* (Cambridge: Harvard University Press, 1930), pp. 71–72.

13. Brickman, "John Dewey's Foreign Reputation as an Educator," pp. 258–259.

14. Jane M. Dewey, "Biography of John Dewey," *The Philosophy of John Dewey*, ed. Paul A. Schilpp (Evanston: Northwestern University, 1939), p. 29.

15. Addams, *Twenty Years at Hull House*, p. 435.

16. Jane M. Dewey, "Biography of John Dewey," p. 30.

17. Lucy L. W. Wilson, *The New Schools of New Russia* (New York: Vanguard, 1928), p. 14.

18. S. Shatzky, "The First Experimental Station of Public Education of the People's Commissariat of Education, U. S. S. R.," *New Era*, IX (January, 1928), 13.

19. Woody, *New Minds*, pp. 47–48.

20. Shatzky, "First Experimental Station," p. 13, and Wilson, *New Schools*, p. 14.

21. Dzh. Diyui, *Shkola i obshchestvo*, ed. I. Gorbunov-Posadov (Moscow: Mosrednik, 1907).

22. Dzh. Diyui, *Psikhologiya i pedagogika mishleniya*, trans. N. M. Nikolskii, ed. N. D. Vinogradov (Moscow: Mir, 1915).

23. Luigi Volpicelli, *Storia della Scuola Sovietica* (Brescia: La Scuola, 1951), p. 29.

24. Scott Nearing, *Education in Soviet Russia* (New York: International Publishers, 1926), p. 8; Sergius Hessen and Nikolaus Hans, *Fünfzehn Jahre des Sowjetschulwesens* (Langensalza: Beltz, 1933), p. 83.

25. N. K. Krupskaya, *Izbrannye pedagogicheskie proizvedeniya* (Moscow: Izdatelstvo Akademii Pedagogicheskikh Nauk R. S. F. S. R., 1955), pp. 40, 152, 205–206.

26. Beatrice King, *Changing Man: The Education System of the U. S. S. R.* (New York: Viking, 1937), p. 20.

27. Adolph E. Meyer, "Soviet Education Turns Right," *American Mercury*, XXXVII (January, 1936), p. 82.

28. Ruth Widmayer, "The End

of American Influence in Soviet Schools," reprint from *Social Studies*, April, 1952, p. 2.

29. Samuel Chester Parker, *A Textbook in the History of Modern Elementary Education: With Emphasis on School Practice in Relation to Social Conditions* (Boston: Ginn, 1912), p. 474.

30. *Ibid.*

31. Nearing, *Education in Russia*, p. 8.

32. Beatrice Ensor, "The Outlook Tower," *New Era*, IX (January, 1928), 5.

33. Lucy L. W. Wilson, *The New Schools*, p. 22.

34. Dzh. Diyui and E. Diyui, *Shkoli budushchego*, trans. P. Landsberg (Moscow, 1918).

35. Dzh. Diyui, *Psikhologiya i pedagogika mishleniya* (Moscow, 1919).

36. Dzh. Diyui, *Shkola i obshchestvo* (Kaluga: Kooperativ Uchashchiksya, 1920).

37. Dzh. Diyui, *Vvednie v filosofiyu vospitaniya*, trans. S. Shatskii. (Moscow, 1921).

38. Dzh. Diyui, *Psikhologiya i pedagogika mishleniya*, trans. N. M. Nikolski, ed. N. D. Vinogradov. (Berlin: Gosizdat, 1922).

39. Dzh. Diyui and E. Diyui, *Shkoli budushchego*, trans. R. Landsberg (Berlin: Gosizdat, 1922).

40. Dzh. Diyui, *Shkola i obshchestvo*, trans. S. T. Shatskii (Moscow: Rabotnik Prosveshcheniya, 1923).

41. Dzh. Diyui, *Shkola i rebenok*, trans. L. Azarevich. (Moscow: Gosizdat, 1922; also 1923). This is apparently a translation of *The School and the Child*, ed. J. J. Findlay (London: Blackie, [1907]), consisting of Dewey's *The Child and the Curriculum* and eight essays from the *Elementary School Record*.

42. Dzh. Diyui, *Shkola i obsh-*

chestvo, trans. G. A. Luchinskii. (Moscow: Rabotnik Prosveshcheniya, 1924; also 1925).

43. At the end of the three-column article on "Diyui (Dewey), Dzhon," *Bolshaya Sovetskaya Entsiklopediya* (Moscow: Ogiz, 1931), XXIII, 720, four translations of Dewey's pedagogical works, none later than 1925, are appended.

44. Anna Louise Strong, "Education in Modern Russia," *Progressive Education,* I (October–November–December, 1924), 158.

45. Harper, "The Russia I Believe In," p. 154.

46. Here the sub-title incorrectly precedes the title. The book was published by the Izdanie Azerbaidzhanskogo Gosudarstvennogo Universiteta imeni V. I. Lenina, the Press of the Lenin State University of Azerbaijan.

47. Quoted in Woody, *New Minds,* p. 49.

48. Leonard Froese, *Ideengeschichtliche Triebkräfte der russischen und sowjetischen Pädagogik* (Heidelberg: Quelle und Meyer, 1956), p. 108.

49. Quoted in Woody, *New Minds,* p. 49.

50. *Ibid.*

51. P. P. Blonskii, *Die Arbeitsschule* (Berlin, 1921), as cited in Froese, *Triebkräfte,* p. 110.

52. Brickman, in *The Changing Soviet School,* pp. 62–64.

53. *Ibid.,* p. 77.

54. *Cf.,* William H. Kilpatrick, "Dewey's Influence on Education," *The Philosophy of John Dewey,* p. 471.

55. Albert P. Pinkevich, *The New Education in the Soviet Republic* (New York: John Day, 1929), p. vi.

56. *Ibid.,* p. 163.

57. *Ibid.*

58. *Ibid.,* p. 177.

59. Brickman, in *The Changing Soviet School,* p. 72.

60. *Pedagogicheskaya Entsiklopediya*, eds., A. G. Kalashnikov and M. S. Epshtein (Moscow: Rabotnik Prosveshcheniya, 1927), I, 6, 334, 422–423, 498, 504, 540, 574, 695.

61. "American Educators in Russia," *School and Society*, XXVII (June 30, 1928), 779. The account in this paragraph is based upon this news story.

62. *Ibid.*

63. See the announcement in Lucy Branham, "An Invitation," *The Nation*, CXXVII (November 14, 1928), 520.

64. Jane Dewey, "Biography of John Dewey," p. 42.

65. "Letters of John Dewey to Robert V. Daniels, 1946–1950," ed. Robert V. Daniels, *Journal of the History of Ideas*, XX (Oct.–Dec., 1959), 573.

66. John Dewey, *Impressions of Soviet Russia and the Revolutionary World: Mexico—China—Turkey* (New York: New Republic, 1929). Dewey's impressions were reprinted in the two volumes of *Characters and Events* (1929), edited by Joseph Ratner.

67. *E.g.*, "Religion in the Soviet Union: II—An Interpretation of the Conflict," *Current History*, XXXII (April, 1930), 31–36.

68. Dewey, *Impressions of Soviet Russia*, p. 6.

69. *Ibid.*, p. 8.

70. *Ibid.*, pp. 14–15.

71. *Ibid.*, p. 15, n.

72. *Ibid.*, p. 17.

73. *Ibid.*, p. 18.

74. *Ibid.*, p. 20.

75. *Ibid.*, p. 24.

76. *Ibid.*, p. 25.

77. *Ibid.*, p. 29.

78. *Ibid.*, p. 28.

79. *Ibid.*, pp. 28–29.

80. *Ibid.*, p. 30.

81. *Ibid.*

82. *Ibid.*, p. 31. *Cf.*, pp. 44–45.

83. *Ibid.*, p. 32.

84. *Ibid.*, p. 33.

85. *Ibid.*, p. 33–34.

86. *Ibid.*, p. 54.

87. *Ibid.*, pp. 60–65, 69–71.

88. *Ibid.*, p. 65.

89. *Ibid.*, p. 69.

90. *Ibid.*, p. 76.

91. *Ibid.*, p. 78.

92. *Ibid.*, p. 80.

93. *Ibid.*, pp. 81–82.

94. *Ibid.*, p. 82.

95. Lenin, quoted *ibid.*, pp. 82–83.

96. *Ibid.*, p. 86.

97. *Ibid.*, p. 93.

98. *Ibid.*, p. 94.

99. *Ibid.*

100. Joseph V. Stalin, *Marksizm i natsionalno-kolonialny vopros* (Moscow, 1938), p. 158, quoted in Frederick C. Barghoorn, *Soviet Russian Nationalism* (New York: Oxford University Press, 1956), p. 19. The dictionary renders the slogan as "Kultura natsionalnaya po forme, sotsialisticheskaya po soderzhaniyu" (Culture national in form, Socialist in content). A. L. Smirnitskii, *Russko-Angliiskii slovar* (Moscow, 1958), p. 737.

101. *Ibid.*, pp. 19–20.

102. Dewey, *Impressions of Soviet Russia*, pp. 96–97.

103. *Ibid.*, p. 97.

104. *Ibid.*, pp. 105–106.

105. *Ibid.*, pp. 106–107.

106. *Ibid.*, pp. 107–108.

107. *Ibid.*, pp. 125–126.

108. *Ibid.*, pp. 128–129.

109. Jane Dewey, "Biography of John Dewey," p. 43. Professor George S. Counts, a younger colleague of Dewey who had a superior knowledge of the Soviet Union and of the Russian language, was also "denounced as a Communist." *Cf.*, "Letters from Dewey to Daniels," p. 573.

110. Martin S. Dworkin, *Dewey on Education* (New York: Bureau of Publications, Teachers College, Columbia University, 1959), p. 11.

111. Dewey, *Impressions of Soviet Russia*, p. 131.

112. Adolph E. Meyer, *John Dewey and Modern Education* (New York: Avon Press, 1931), p. 56.
113. Salomon M. Teitelbaum, "The Dalton Plan in the Soviet Schools," *Harvard Educational Review*, XVII (Spring, 1947), 92.
114. Adolph E. Meyer, *The Development of Education in the Twentieth Century*, 2d ed. (New York: Prentice-Hall, 1949), p. 489.
115. Pinkevich, *The New Education*, p. 285.
116. Quoted in Teitelbaum, "The Dalton Plan," p. 97.
117. B. B. Komarovskii, *Filosofiskie predposilki pedagogiki Diyui* (Baku: Izvestiya Azerbaidzhanskogo Gosudarstvennogo Universiteta imeni V. I. Lenina, 1926). This was not available to the writer.
118. B. B. Komarovskii, *Sovremennie pedagogicheskie techeniya: Tom I, Filosofiya vospitaniya Dzhona Diyui v svyazi s istorei amerikanskoi pedagogiki* (Baku: Izdanie Azerbaidzhanskogo Gosudarstvennogo Universiteta imeni V. I. Lenina, 1930).
119. *Ibid.*, pp. 216–218.
120. *Ibid.*, pp. 226–234.
121. *Ibid.*, pp. 234–240.
122. *Ibid.*, p. 234.
123. *Ibid.*
124. *Ibid.*, pp. 234–235.
125. *Ibid.*, p. 235.
126. *Ibid.*
127. "Diyui (Dewey), Dzhon," *Sovetskaya Entsiklopediya*, XXIII (1931). The translations quoted in this paragraph are from Martin Levit, "Soviet Version of John Dewey and Pragmatism," *History of Education Journal*, IV (Summer, 1953), 137–138.
128. Quoted in Levit, "John Dewey and Pragmatism," p. 137.
129. Quoted *ibid.*, pp. 137–138.
130. Quoted *ibid.*, p. 138.
131. *Ibid.*, pp. 136–137.
132. The full text of the resolu-

tion is in *Khrestomatiya po istorii pedagogiki*, V. Z. Smirnov ed. (Moscow: Uchpedgiz, 1957), pp. 449–457. For an English translation, see I. L. Kandel, "The Educational Merry-Go-Round in Soviet Russia," *Kadelpian Review*, May 1935, pp. 328–330.
133. Albert P. Pinkevich, *Science and Education in the U. S. S. R.* (London: Gollancz, 1935), p. 40.
134. Teitelbaum, "The Dalton Plan," p. 99.
135. The full Russian text of this decree is in Smirnov, *Khrestomatiya*, pp. 457–464.
136. Quoted in Michael Demiashkevich, *An Introduction to the Philosophy of Education* (New York: American Book Company, 1935), p. 185.
137. *New York Herald Tribune*, Sept. 3, 1933, dispatch from Moscow.
138. Quoted in Demiashkevich, *Introduction to the Philosophy of Education*, p. 188. The English text of this decree is on pp. 186–188.
139. *New York Herald Tribune*, Sept. 3, 1933.
140. *Ibid.*
141. Brickman, in *The Changing Soviet School*, p. 70.
142. English translations of the decrees are in Kandel, "The Educational Merry-Go-Round," pp. 332–333.
143. The full Russian text is in Smirnov, *Khrestomatiya*, pp. 464–468.
144. A. Gilenson, "The Teachers of the U. S. S. R. Fifteen Years after the October Revolution," *Soviet Culture Review* (Moscow: Voks, 1932), No. 7–9, p. 41.
145. Brickman, in *The Changing Soviet School*, p. 72.
146. The Russian text is in Smirnov, *Khrestomatiya*, pp. 468–472.
147. Raymond A. Bauer, *The*

New Man in Soviet Psychology (Cambridge: Harvard University Press, 1952), pp. 123–127.

148. Clyde W. Park, *Ambassador to Industry: The Idea and Life of Herman Schneider* (Indianapolis: Bobbs-Merrill, 1953), pp. 251–254. The first name of Pinkevich is erroneously given as Paul.

149. Smirnov, *Khrestomatiya,* p. 494. *Cf.,* N. A. Konstantinov and V. Z. Smirnov, *Istoriya pedagogiki* (Moscow: Uchpedgiz, 1955), pp. 215–222.

150. Frederic Lilge, *Anton Semyonovich Makarenko: An Analysis of His Educational Ideas in the Context of Soviet Society* (Berkeley: University of California Press, 1958), p. 2.

151. *Ibid.,* p. 4.

152. *Ibid.*

153. Brickman, in *The Changing Soviet School,* p. 73.

154. Meyer, "Soviet Education Turns Right," p. 84.

155. *Ibid.*

156. *Ibid.,* p. 85.

157. Nina M. Sorochenko, "Pre-School Education in the U. S. S. R.," *Soviet Education,* ed. George L. Kline (New York: Columbia University Press, 1957), p. 6.

158. *Ibid.,* p. 12.

159. This account of Trotsky's exile is based on Georg von Rauch, *Geschichte des bolschewistischen Russland* (Wiesbaden: Rheinische Verlags-Anstalt, 1955), *passim.*

160. James T. Farrell, "Dewey in Mexico," *John Dewey: Philosopher of Science and Freedom,* ed. Sidney Hook (New York: Dial, 1950), p. 357.

161. *Ibid.*

162. Sidney Hook, "Some Memories of John Dewey: 1859–1952," *Commentary,* XIV (September, 1952), 250.

163. *Ibid.,* p. 251. Farrell, "Dewey in Mexico," p. 357.

164. Hook, "Some Memories of John Dewey," p. 250.

165. John Dewey, *"Truth Is on the March": Report and Remarks on the Trotsky Hearings in Mexico* (New York: American Committee for the Defense of Leon Trotsky, [1937]), p. 5.

166. Quoted in Farrell, "Dewey in Mexico," p. 362.

167. Quoted *ibid.*

168. Quoted *ibid.,* p. 368.

169. *Ibid.,* p. 365.

170. *Ibid.,* p. 371.

171. Quoted *ibid.,* p. 374.

172. John Dewey, *"Truth Is on the March,"* p. 9.

173. *Ibid.,* p. 10.

174. *Ibid.,* p. 13.

175. *Ibid.,* p. 12.

176. *Ibid.*

177. *Ibid.,* p. 14.

178. *Ibid.,* p. 15.

179. *Ibid.*

180. Quoted *ibid.*

181. *Ibid.,* pp. 7–8.

182. Agnes E. Meyer, "Significance of the Trotsky Trial: Interview with John Dewey," *International Conciliation,* February, 1938, p. 54. Reprinted from the *Washington Post,* December 19, 1937.

183. Quoted in Farrell, "Dewey in Mexico," pp. 375–376.

184. Quoted *ibid.,* p. 376.

185. Quoted in Agnes E. Meyer, "Interview with John Dewey."

186. Quoted *ibid.,* p. 55.

187. Quoted *ibid.*

188. Quoted *ibid.,* p. 56.

189. Hook, "Some Memories of John Dewey," p. 257.

190. Quoted in Agnes Meyer, "Interview with John Dewey," pp. 56–57.

191. Quoted *ibid.,* p. 57.

192. Quoted *ibid.,* pp. 59–60.

193. Farrell, "Dewey in Mexico," p. 375.

194. *Ibid.,* p. 376.

195. *Ibid.,* pp. 376–377.

196. *Ibid.,* p. 377.

197. V. J. McGill, "Pragmatism Reconsidered: An Aspect of John Dewey's Philosophy," *Science and Society*, III (Summer, 1939), 322.

198. Robert W. Iversen, *The Communists and the Schools* (New York: Harcourt, Brace, 1959), p. 157.

199. *Ibid.*, p. 87.

200. *Ibid.*, p. 86.

201. *Ibid.*

202. *Ibid.*, pp. 86–87. (quoted from *The Modern Monthly* [April, 1934], 137).

203. John Dewey, "From Absolutism to Experimentalism," *Contemporary American Philosophy: Personal Statements*, ed. George P. Adams and William Pepperell Montague (London: Allen and Unwin 1930), Vol. II, p. 19.

204. *Ibid.*, p. 20.

205. *Ibid.*, p. 21.

206. *Ibid.*

207. John Dewey, *Individualism Old and New* (New York: Minton Balch, 1930), p. 95.

208. *Ibid.*, p. 118.

209. *Cf.*, George R. Geiger, *John Dewey in Perspective* (New York: Oxford University Press, 1958), p. 182.

210. Sidney Hook, *John Dewey: An Intellectual Portrait* (New York: John Day, 1939), p. 165.

211. *Ibid.*, p. 158.

212. Quoted in Jim Cork, "John Dewey and Karl Marx," *John Dewey: Philosopher of Science and Freedom*, ed. Sidney Hook (New York: Dial Press, 1950), p. 349.

213. Quoted *ibid.*

214. John Dewey, *Liberalism and Social Action* (New York: Putnam, 1935), pp. 86–87.

215. John Dewey, *Freedom and Culture* (New York: Putnam, 1939), pp. 77–102.

216. *Ibid.*, p. 87.

217. *Ibid.*, p. 101.

218. *Ibid.*, pp. 89–90.

219. *Ibid.*, p. 71.

220. John Dewey, "Experience, Knowledge and Value: A Rejoinder," in *The Philosophy of John Dewey*, pp. 593–594.

221. *Ibid.*, p. 607.

222. Cork, "Dewey and Marx," p. 341. For the similarities between Marx and Dewey, see pp. 338–341.

223. *Ibid.*, p. 348.

224. *Ibid.*, p. 335.

225. *Ibid.*, p. 337.

226. Geiger, *Dewey in Perspective*, p. 181.

227. *Ibid.*, p. 179.

228. John Herman Randall, Jr., "Dewey's Interpretation of the History of Philosophy," in *The Philosophy of John Dewey*, p. 88.

229. Hook, "Some Memories of John Dewey," p. 251.

230. John Dewey, Letter to the Editor, *New York Times*, January 11, 1942, quoted in Iversen, *The Communists and the Schools*, p. 229.

231. Quoted *ibid.*, p. 230.

232. For criticizing this film, Dewey was labeled a "Trotskyite." See Letter of November 17, 1947, in "Letters of Dewey to Daniels," p. 572.

233. *E.g.*, E. N. Medynskii, *Istoriya pedagogiki*, 2d ed. (Moscow: Gosudarstvennoye Uchebno-pedagogicheskoe Izdatelstvo Narkomprosa, R. S. F. S. R., 1941), Vol. I, 379–482, 504.

234. *Cf.*, George S. Counts and Nucia Lodge, *The Country of the Blind: The Soviet System of Mind Control* (Boston: Houghton Mifflin, 1949), pp. 254–255.

235. *Ibid.*, p. 84.

236. *Pravda*, November 25, 1946, quoted *ibid.*, p. 155. The description of Stalin as "the greatest scholar of our epoch" is quoted on p. 156.

237. *Sovetskaya Pedagogika*, December, 1946, p. 3, quoted *ibid.*, p. 260.

238. *Sovetskaya Pedagogika*, Oc-

tober–November, 1946, pp. 3–8, quoted *ibid.*, p. 259.

239. *Ibid.*

240. *Sovetskaya Pedagogika,* September, 1947, p. 30, quoted *ibid.*, p. 261.

241. *Sovetskaya Pedagogika,* February, 1948, p. 10, quoted *ibid.*

242. *Sovetskaya Pedagogika,* October, 1947, p. 84, as quoted *ibid.*

243. *Ibid.*

244. A. G. Kalashnikov, *Thirty Years of Soviet Education* (Moscow, 1947), (in Russian) quoted *ibid.*, p. 264.

245. Quoted *ibid.*, p. 265.

246. Quoted *ibid.*

247. Quoted *ibid.*, p. 270.

248. Quoted *ibid.*, p. 271.

249. *Ibid.*, p. 277. The original Dewey source is cited on p. 278.

250. *Ibid.*, p. 275.

251. *Ibid.*, p. 274.

252. *Biographical Directory of the U. S. S. R.,* ed. Wladimir S. Merzalow (New York: Scarecrow Press, 1958), p. 240.

253. Quoted in Levit, *John Dewey and Pragmatism,* pp. 139–140.

254. V. A. Veikshan, "Idealism and Mysticism in English Pedagogy," *Sovetskaya Pedagogika,* February, 1948, p. 114. This reference was made available in English by Professor Martin Levit of the University of Kansas City. All but the description of Dewey is quoted in Levit, *John Dewey and Pragmatism,* p. 140.

255. N. A. Konstantinov, *30 Jahre Sowjetpädagogik* (Berlin: Volk und Wissen Verlag, 1948), p. 8. The original Russian article was published in *Sovetskaya Pedagogika,* February, 1948.

256. P. A. Oreschkow, *Die Grundlagen der sowjetischen Didaktik* (Berlin: Volk und Wissen Verlag, 1948), p. 36.

257. E. N. Medinskii, "Sovetskaya shkola v R. S. F. S. R. v

1921–1929 godakh," *Ocherki po istorii sovetskoi shkoli R. S. F. S. R. za 30 let,* eds. N. A. Konstantinov and E. N. Medinskii (Moscow: Uchpedgiz, 1948), p. 98.

258. Counts and Lodge, *The Country of the Blind,* pp. 313–14.

259. *Pravda,* March 26, 1949, quoted, *ibid.*, p. 316.

260. N. K. Goncharov, quoted in George S. Counts, *American Education Through the Soviet Looking Glass* (New York: Bureau of Publications, Teachers College, Columbia University, 1951), p. 22.

261. Quoted *ibid.*

262. Quoted *ibid.*, p. 23.

263. Quoted *ibid.*, p. 24.

264. Quoted *ibid.*, p. 25.

265. Quoted *ibid.*

266. Quoted *ibid.*, p. 35.

267. Quoted *ibid.*, p. 37.

268. Quoted *ibid.*, p. 38.

269. Quoted *ibid.*, p. 39.

270. Quoted *ibid.*, p. 40.

271. Quoted *ibid.*, p. 41.

272. Quoted *ibid.*

273. *Ibid.*, p. 6.

274. *Ibid.*, p. 42.

275. *Ibid.*, pp. 42–43.

276. *Ibid.*, p. 48.

277. *Ibid.*

278. George S. Counts, *The Challenge of Soviet Education* (New York: McGraw-Hill, 1957), p. 188.

279. B. P. Yesipov and N. K. Goncharov, *I Want to Be Like Stalin.* Trans. George S. Counts and Nucia P. Lodge (New York: John Day, 1947).

280. Quoted in Levit, *John Dewey and Pragmatism,* p. 140. The present writer could not locate this sentence in the 1940 or 1956 edition (Kairov-Goncharov-Yesipov-Zankov), nor in the German translation of the 1946 edition.

281. "Diyui (Dewey) Dzhon," *Sovetskaya Entsiklopediya,* 2d ed. (1952), pp. 343–344, as quoted in

Levit, *John Dewey and Pragmatism*, pp. 138–139.
282. Quoted *ibid.*, p. 139.
283. Quoted *ibid.*
284. *Ibid.*, p. 138.
285. V. S. Shevkin, *Pedagogika D. Diyui na sluzhbe sovremennoi Amerikanskoi reaktsii* (Moscow: Uchpedgiz, 1952), p. 31. All translations from the Russian were made by the present writer.
286. *Ibid.*, p. 22.
287. *Ibid.*, p. 30.
288. *Ibid.*, p. 32.
289. *Ibid.*, p. 34.
290. *Ibid.*, p. 53.
291. *Ibid.*, p. 61.
292. *Ibid.*, p. 69.
293. *Ibid.*, p. 71.
294. *Ibid.*, p. 75.
295. *Ibid.*, p. 89.
296. *Ibid.*, p. 91.
297. *Ibid.*, p. 99.
298. *Ibid.*, p. 95.
299. *Ibid.*, pp. 103, 108, 109.
300. *Ibid.*, pp. 116, 120.
301. *Ibid.*, p. 121.
302. *Ibid.*, p. 125.
303. *Ibid.*, p. 135.
304. *Ibid.*, p. 138.
305. *Ibid.*, p. 141.
306. *Ibid.*, p. 140.
307. *Ibid.*, p. 142.
308. W. S. Schewkin, *Die Pädagogik J. Deweys* (Berlin: Volk und Wissen Verlag, 1955).
309. Corliss Lamont, *Soviet Civilization* (New York: Philosophical Library, 1952), p. 226.
310. I. V. Chuvashev, *Ocherki po istorii doshkolnogo vospitaniya v Rossii* (Moscow: Uchpedgiz, 1955), p. 295.
311. M. A. Danilov and B. P. Yesipov, *Didaktika* (Moscow: Izdatelstvo Akademii Pedagogicheskikh Nauk, 1957), p. 31.
312. S. T. Shatskii, "Moi pedagogicheskii put," *S. T. Shatskii v ego pedagogicheskikh viskazivaniyakh,* ed. S. A. Cherepanov (Moscow: Uchpedgiz, 1958), pp. 19, 22.
313. S. T. Shatskii, "Moi pedagogicheskii put," *S. T. Shatskii: Izbrannie pedagogicheskie sochineniya,* eds. A. N. Volkovskii *et al.* (Moscow: Uchpedgiz, 1958), p. 419. Pp. 19–20 of Shatskii's essay in the Cherepanov monograph were omitted.
314. F. F. Korolev, *Ocherki po istorii sovetskoi shkoli i pedagogiki: 1917–20* (Moscow: Izdatelstvo Akademii Pedagogicheskikh Nauk R. S. F. S. R., 1958), p. 320.
315. Z. I. Ravkin, *Sovetskaya shkola v period vosstanovleniya narodnogo chozyaistva: 1921–1925 gg.* (Moscow: Uchpedgiz, 1959), pp. 135–138.
316. N. K. Goncharov, "Sovetskaya pedagogika k 40-letiyu velikovo Oktyabra," *Sovetskaya Pedagogika,* XXI (November 1957), pp. 38–39.
317. *Istoriya pedagogika* 2d ed., ed. M. F. Shabaeva (Moscow: Uchpedgiz, 1955), p. 198.
318. A. S. Bubnov, *Stati i rechi o narodnom obrazovanii* (Moscow: Izdatelstvo Akademii Pedagogicheskikh Nauk R. S. F. S. R., 1959), pp. 178–273.
319. *Sovetskaya istoriko-pedagogicheskaya literatura (1918–57): Sistematicheskii ukazatel,* ed. A. I. Piskunov (Moscow: Izdatelstvo Akademii Pedagogicheskikh Nauk R. S. F. S. R., 1960), pp. 80–81.
320. "Diyui (Dewey), Dzhon (1859–1952)," *Pedagogicheskii slovar,* eds. I. A. Kairov and N. K. Goncharov (Moscow: Izdatelstvo Pedagogicheskikh Nauk R. S. F. S. R., 1960), I, 362.
321. *Ibid.*, p. 363.
322. Isaac Deutscher, *The Great Contest: Russia and the West* (New York: Oxford University Press, 1960) pp. 27–28.
323. Thomas Berry, C. P., "Dewey's Influence in China," *John Dewey: His Thought and*

Influence, ed. John Blewett, S. J. (New York: Fordham University Press, 1960), p. 200. The account of Dewey in China has been most thoroughly treated by Berry, pp. 199–232. See also Fung Yu-Lan, *A Short History of Chinese Philosophy* (New York: Macmillan, 1948), p. 329.

324. Benjamin I. Schwartz, *Chinese Communism and the Rise of Mao* (Cambridge: Harvard University Press, 1951), p. 19. See also pp. 20, 22, 23.

325. Berry, "Dewey's Influence in China," p. 208.

326. *Ibid.,* p. 214.

327. *Ibid.,* p. 224.

328. Theodore H. E. Chen, *Thought Reform of the Chinese Intellectuals* (Hong Kong: Hong Kong University Press, 1960), p. 44.

329. *Ibid.,* p. 49.

330. *Jen-min jih-pao,* January 19, 1955, quoted *ibid.,* p. 84.

331. Brickman, "John Dewey's Foreign Reputation," pp. 257–265 and "John Dewey: Educator of Nations," pp. 132–143.

332. Z. Malkova, "Budte obyektivni, kollegi: Otkritoe pismo v Ameriku," *Uchitelskaya Gazeta,* October 4, 1960. See the English translation, "An Open Letter to America: Be Objective, Colleagues!" *Comparative Education Review,* V (June 1961), 69–72, and the reply by the present writer, "The Objectivity of a Soviet Pedagogue," *ibid.,* 72–73.

333. James T. Farrell, *Reflections at Fifty and other Essays* (New York: Vanguard, 1954), p. 30.

INDEX